## PRAISE FOR *THE UPSTA...*

"Memoir, thoughts about food, and literary criticism are stacked, in *The Upstairs Delicatessen*, like the bright layers of a Venetian cookie."

—Alexandra Schwartz, *The New Yorker*

"This is one of my favorite books of all time."

—Christopher Kimball, *Milk Street Radio*

"*The Upstairs Delicatessen*, [Garner's] delightful, quote-stuffed memoir, tracks the evolution of his reading habits ('Autobiography, for me, quickly edges into bibliography') and pairs that appetite with another, for food . . . What makes it as satisfying as that midnight cheeseburger . . . is the same formula that keeps Garner's reviews fresh and entertaining week after week: his eagerness to amuse and the rolling canter of his prose—embellished, always, by his notorious addiction to metaphor."

—Adam Begley, *The Times Literary Supplement*

"Dwight Garner is a food writer . . . and perhaps that is too limiting a term for him . . . of the first order!"

—Norman Van Aken

"[A] marvelous edible memoir . . . Each of Garner's perfectly selected morsels affirms the importance of writing and eating well."          —Jessica Carbone, *Gastronomica*

Richard Bowditch

DWIGHT GARNER

# THE UPSTAIRS DELICATESSEN

Dwight Garner is a book critic for *The New York Times* and was previously the senior editor of *The New York Times Book Review*. His essays and criticism have also appeared in *The New Republic*, *Harper's Magazine*, *Slate*, and other publications. He is the author of *Garner's Quotations*.

# THE **UPSTAIRS DELICATESSEN**

On Eating, Reading,
Reading About Eating,
and Eating While Reading

# **DWIGHT GARNER**

PICADOR • FARRAR, STRAUS AND GIROUX
NEW YORK

Picador
120 Broadway, New York 10271

Owing to limitations of space, all acknowledgments for permission to reprint previously published material can be found on pages 241–244.

Interior art by spiral media / Shutterstock.com.

The Library of Congress has cataloged the Farrar, Straus and Giroux hardcover edition as follows:
Names: Garner, Dwight, author.
Title: The upstairs delicatessen: on eating, reading, reading about eating, and eating while reading / Dwight Garner.
Description: First edition. | New York : Farrar, Straus and Giroux, 2023. | Includes index.
Identifiers: LCCN 2023014918 | ISBN 9780374603427 (hardcover)
Subjects: LCSH: Garner, Dwight. | Critics—United States—Biography. | Food habits. | Books and reading. | LCGFT: Autobiographies.
Classification: LCC PN75.G37 A3 2023 | DDC 818/.603—dc23/eng/20230623
LC record available at https://lccn.loc.gov/2023014918

Paperback ISBN: 978-1-250-33836-5

*Designed by Gretchen Achilles*

Our books may be purchased in bulk for promotional, educational, or business use. Please contact your local bookseller or the Macmillan Corporate and Premium Sales Department at 1-800-221-7945, extension 5442, or by email at MacmillanSpecialMarkets@macmillan.com.

For book club information, please email marketing@picadorusa.com.

picadorusa.com • Follow us on social media at @picador or @picadorusa

1   3   5   7   9   10   8   6   4   2

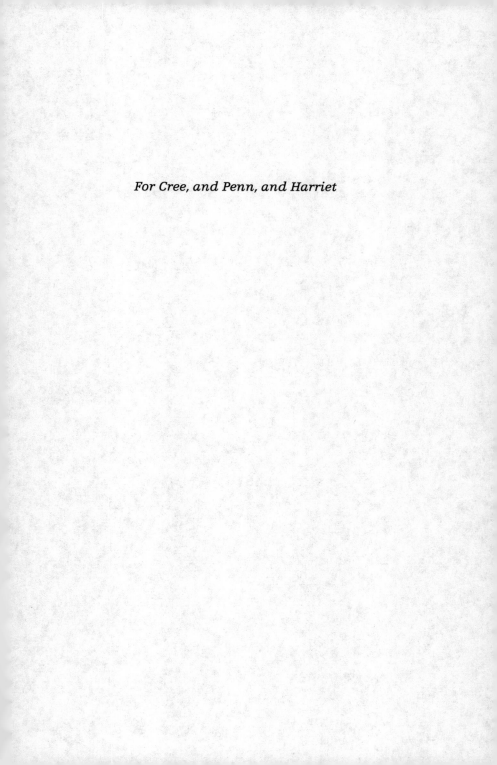

*For Cree, and Penn, and Harriet*

Love isn't saying "I love you" but calling to say "did you eat?"

—MARLON JAMES

There is no great difference between novels and banana bread. They are both just something to do.
—ZADIE SMITH, *Intimations*

I'd rather smoke crack than eat cheese from a can.
—GWYNETH PALTROW

**Q:** What do you do when your mind goes blank?
**A:** Go to the refrigerator and eat.
—VIVIAN GORNICK, *Paris Review* interview

I want, I want, I want.
—SAUL BELLOW, *Henderson the Rain King*

# CONTENTS

# INTRODUCTION

For Henry, reading had always been a gentle thing, a thing as delicate as blowing eggs. Two pinpricks and the meaning came, whole, unbroken, into the bowl.

**—ALLEGRA GOODMAN**, *The Family Markowitz*

When I was young, growing up in West Virginia and then in southwest Florida, I was a soft kid, inclined toward embonpoint, "husky" in the department-store lingo, a brown-eyed boy with chafing thighs because I liked to eat while I read—and, reader, I read whatever was handy. George Orwell described his childhood self as having a "large, rather fat face, with big jowls, a bit like a hamster." This was my look, too, so much so that my friends presented me with a hamster as a joke gift. I regret to inform you that I named it Holden, after J. D. Salinger's hero. Holden ate lettuce and, probably despairing of his diet, staggered backward theatrically on his hind legs one day and croaked, like Lee Marvin in *The Man Who Shot Liberty Valance*.

I was eight when we moved south. My parents were in flight from West Virginia's long, isolating winters. They were done carrying pots of boiling water out to dump over ice-sealed car doors. I spent my first week in Naples miserable, uprooted, in exile, missing my friends, intermittently weeping, sometimes performatively, and listening nonstop to the first record I'd ever asked for: John Denver's new one, *Poems, Prayers & Promises*, with "Take Me Home, Country Roads" on side two. Here was my plight, articulated exactly, a rare thing at any age. I already missed West Virginia's mountains and the way the weather boiled up from them. I missed the way the light is dealt out through the peaks. I was even homesick for Charleston's paper-mill reek and the stacks of rusted cars and refrigerators in the valleys that one politician called "jumbled jungles of junkery." Naples, on the other hand, popped like a postcard. I didn't trust it. There was something predatory (all those alligators eyeballing you from the ponds) and flimsy about every sun-splashed, underground sprinkler–mined, golf course–adjacent acre. Cynthia Ozick would write, "The whole peninsula of Florida was weighted down with regret. Everyone had left behind a real life."

I attended Saint Ann, a middle school with a Catholic church attached. The girls wore plaid skirts and short-sleeved white dress shirts; boys wore dark trousers and strangely casual teal T-shirts. It took me a long time to find friends. When classes began, so did a daily ritual that became the most important thing in my life. I'd bicycle home under the Gulf Coast sun, sizzled crisp and pink with sweat, gather an armload of newspapers and magazines and library books and paperback novels, and heave this bundle onto the carpet of the living room floor. My family's ranch-style house had jalousie windows but no air-conditioning; a ceiling fan churned overhead; mosquitoes, hell-bent little fuckers, vectored in the downdraft. Their blood—*my* blood—blotted the spots where I smashed them.

Reading material acquired, part two of my ritual fell into place. I'd toddle into the kitchen. Ten minutes later I'd return with a sandwich, sodden with mayonnaise, cheese slices poking out like a stealth bomber's wings, as well as vertiginous piles of potato chips and pretzels and a cold red drink made from powder mix. To this day, I find the cuboid bits of crunchy salt at the bottom of certain pretzel bags almost unholy in their deliciousness, worthy of cutting on a mirror, snorting, and rubbing on the gumline. I'd read on my stomach, chin cupped in my right hand, the pages pushed out in front of me. It was important that the food not run out before the newspapers and books did. I'd return for more chips so I could make a clean sweep of the *Miami Herald* sports pages. That newspaper's sports columnist, Edwin Pope, was the first critic who mattered to me. I'd stagger back to the kitchen for a sleeve of Hydrox cookies* and milk, enough to propel me through half of a crime novel by Boston's Robert B. Parker. His hero, Spenser, was a hard guy with a soft touch in the kitchen, a rare combo platter back then. "Spenser's the name," he'd say, "cooking's the game." He tangled with bad guys yet knew his way around knobs of ginger and paws of garlic. Sometimes, too, after school, I'd flip through a skin magazine, *Club* or *Chic* or *Oui*, found in the weeds by the side of the road; someone no doubt had tossed it from a car window and probably regretted it later. I read these alone in my room, not eating a bite. I remember a *Penthouse Forum* letter in which a woman described doing things with mashed potatoes, gravy, and her grateful boyfriend that made me look at side dishes with fresh eyes.

Hermione Lee, the English biographer, has distinguished between two types of reading, "vertical" and "horizontal." The

---

* In *Underworld*, Don DeLillo writes: "All the other kids ate Oreo cookies. Eric ate Hydrox cookies because the name sounded like rocket fuel."

first is "regulated, supervised, orderly, canonical and productive." The second and more intimate variety is "unlicensed, private, leisurely, disreputable, promiscuous and anarchic." Our real reading tends to be of the latter variety. On that living room floor, I turned from Parker, for whom I maintain a real fondness, toward more ambitious writers, the kind that slowly put me at a certain distance from my family and peers. I'd tattoo the pages with greasy fingerprints. My bouts of afternoon grazing could last three or four hours. They were irritating to my father, who like most fathers would have preferred to see his son outside in shoulder pads. I was big enough for football, but I didn't have the nature for it. I'd be sure to finish eating and reading before he returned from work. If I heard him approaching, I'd devour the last cookie with a pelican jerk of my neck. I learned a lesson that's crucial to misfits of every stripe: the way to keep a secret is to eat the evidence. My father did not, as the historian Garry Wills's father did, offer to pay me to read less. In his memoir, *Outside Looking In*, Wills writes that he took the money and used it to buy more books.

Reading and eating, like Krazy and Ignatz, *Sturm und Drang*, prosciutto and melon, Simon and Schuster, and radishes and butter, have always, for me, simply gone together. The book you're holding is a ~~cry for help~~ product of these combined gluttonies. While reading, I'm helpless: I always (a) wish I were also eating and (b) notice the food. In this book's five chapters—breakfast, lunch, shopping, drinking, and dinner—I'll walk through a day in the life of an omnidirectionally hungry human being (me), with attention paid to what writers have thought and said about what we put in our mouths and why. I'll rely on my own perceptions, but also on those of the minds whose appetites have informed my own. Autobiography, for me, quickly edges into bibliography. The great critic Seymour Krim liked to refer to his memory as "that profuse upstairs delicatessen of mine." It's a phrase I've always loved. The upstairs delicatessen! We all have one. This book is in no small part about the contents of my own.

I've been happy, over time, to find confirmation that I wasn't alone in my combinatory passion for reading and eating. Rita Dove, in "In the Old Neighborhood," writes about how

> *Candy buttons went with Brenda Starr,*
> *Bazooka bubble gum with the Justice*
> *League of America. Fig Newtons*
> *and* King Lear, *bitter lemon as well*
> *for* Othello, *that desolate*
> *conspicuous soul.*

Frank Conroy, in his memoir *Stop-Time*, recalls lying in bed after his father's early death "with a glass of milk and a package of oatmeal cookies beside me." For consolation he read "one paperback after another until two or three in the morning." Dorothy Allison's *Bastard Out of Carolina* is a reminder that summer is when whole forests can fall to the buzz saw of a young person's reading. Allison's narrator recalls, "When school let out for the summer, I found a hiding place in the woods near Aunt Alma's where I could camp for hours with a bag of Hershey Kisses and a book." The critic Albert Murray described a friend who cut school to binge-read Faulkner's *Light in August*, holing up "Sherlock Holmes style with it and a jug." I've never nursed a jug while reading, but in high school I did find a used bookstore* that didn't mind if you sat on the floor with a six-pack between your outstretched legs and slowly ingested its contents.

We read for tangled, overlapping reasons. I read primarily, I sometimes think, out of an accelerated sense of what Tina Brown, in her *Vanity Fair Diaries*, called "observation greed." I've looked to novels and memoirs and biographies and diaries and cookbooks and books of letters for advice about *how to live*, the way cannibals ate the brains of brilliant captives, seeking to grow brilliant themselves. Often this has meant paying close attention to what, and how, people eat. I'm sympathetic with Elizabeth Hardwick, who got caught up in what she called the "drama of consumption" in Mary McCarthy's novels. I'm beside Jake Barnes in *The Sun Also Rises*, who declares about the world: "I did not care what it was all about. All I wanted to know was how to live in it." Eve Babitz loved Colette's fiction because she's among those writers whose books "you open up anywhere and brush up on what to do." I like Babitz for the same reason. Food in literature— the "drama of consumption"—has always made me turn the pages more briskly. I am equally addicted to cookbooks and food magazines and Substacks and kitchen memoirs, pouncing on them like a flying squirrel upon acorns.

This semi-autobiographical book is in some ways a history of this reading. I believe, alongside the poet Charles Simic,

---

* The Book Trader, in Naples, Florida, now defunct. Its motto, stamped in green ink on the inside cover of each book, was "After you've read it / swap it for credit / at the Book Trader."

that when our souls are happy, they talk about food. It's our real best friend, John Updike informed us, for

> It never bites back;
> it is already dead.
> It never tells us we are lousy lovers
> or asks us for an interview.
> It simply begs, Take me;
> it cries out, I'm yours.

Here's an example of what I mean when I say that I read out of observation greed. In *A View from the Bed*, her exemplary collection of essays, the late English writer Jenny Diski wrote that she was devoted to a type of black Indian tea known as Assam. She called it a "particularly reliable hedge against life's little disappointments." *Jenny*, I remember thinking to myself, *I have little disappointments of my own*. I hadn't heard of Assam, so I found a box. It's strong and dark and mind-focusing, and on many mornings now, I brew a cup. When I do, I think of Diski, whose writing I miss. It's a point of contact. Like teeth, Walter Bagehot wrote, writers are divided into incisors and grinders. Diski was an incisor. Orwell is in my head, too, when I make tea—but that's for another chapter.

Too much food talk, I'm aware, can make a person feel smug and bourgeois. I like Kenneth Tynan's answer, when he was asked how he could call himself a socialist and still eat well. "Good food should be available to everyone," he replied. "Socialism which denies the pleasures of the gullet is Socialism disfigured by the English puritan tradition." I'm aware, too, that not everyone cares about what they put into their mouths. "I have no palate," Lord Byron said. Benjamin Franklin was indifferent to his meals. My friend Charles "Chip" McGrath, when he was editor of *The New York Times Book Review*, would complain there was no pill he could take instead of consuming three meals a day. The architect Louis Kahn so dismissed the importance of meals that, in the houses he designed, the kitchens are notoriously cramped and hard to find. Beryl Bainbridge said she didn't believe in eating and would simply *forget* to do so. (My tall and skinny son forgets, too.) She used to fall over at parties; people assumed she was drunk. The narrator in Karl Ove Knausgaard's *My Struggle* novels speaks for all these people when he announces, "I didn't give a rat's ass about food." Perhaps you're a bit like these hardy souls—though I doubt it, because you're reading this book. You probably agree (as I do) with Thackeray, who wrote that when you brag about not caring about what you eat, you're bragging about a character defect.

When I was growing up in the seventies, neither side of my family put much thought into food; back then, almost no one did. *The Bear*, single-udder butter, and bone marrow pho recipes gone viral were not only decades away but also impossible to imagine. Everyone wasn't a sophisticate. On my father's side were coal miners and gunsmiths, all of them hunters. Their freezers were stuffed with slabs of venison wrapped in waxed paper. Thawed out, this stuff could be funky in its animal reality. It disappeared, meal after meal, beneath the awnings of grateful mustaches. My dad's father, Archie, was a miner who kept ginseng and heartwood and leaves and bark and sharp-smelling herbs and other stump-water cures in his trouser pockets. When someone had a headache or a sore tooth, he'd pull out a few crumpled leaves, hand them to the bewildered sufferer, and say, "Here, chew on these."

Archie spent thirty years in the mines and got out when he was in his fifties. He opened a one-man real estate business out of his home, and he had a knack for it. A Sunday meal at his creaking Victorian house in Mannington, West Virginia, would be prepared by my grandmother Mary, a former schoolteacher, whom we called Nanny. The supper would be anchored by venison or some other kind of roast. There were string beans, cooked in a rattling pressure cooker with a slice of bacon for flavor. We'd topped and tailed the beans earlier on the back porch. There were mashed potatoes, warm rolls, and (always) a serving dish filled with applesauce, sometimes but not always homemade. Archie was a devotee of the health faddist Horace Fletcher (1849–1919), the "Great Masticator," who encouraged people to eat slowly and thoroughly. Archie chewed each bite thirty-two times and sometimes made us do it, too. It's a cruel thing to make a kid do; every bite becomes hateful paste in your mouth. Dessert was Waldorf salad, made with mayonnaise and Jell-O. After dinner, Archie would lean back in his chair, unlatch his belt, and undo the top two buttons on his brown stretch slacks. He'd pat his stomach with both hands and beam with pleasure. It was his way of praising abundance, and of praising the cook. If Nanny loosened her girdle, she did so discreetly, out of eyesight.

Archie had been through the Depression and knew what it was like to do without. He wasted nothing, certainly not tissues. If he needed to blow his nose, he'd go into the bath-room and stand over the sink and turn on both taps. He'd lean over and press a finger to one nostril and empty the other into the sink, and then repeat the performance on the other side. The rushing water flushed these eliminations away. The entire performance, which seemed to me entirely hygienic, took about four seconds. Then he'd warsh (his pro-nunciation) his hands and walk back out. Edna O'Brien, in *The Country Girls*, wrote that a blob of Vicks VapoRub placed on the tongue blots hunger. That's the sort of folk wisdom of which Archie would have approved. Sometimes after dinner he could be coaxed into reciting "The Shooting of Dan Mc-Grew," a long and thrilling ballad by the British-Canadian poet Robert Service, that he had learned by heart.

Archie's side of the family went back centuries in West Vir-ginia. My mother's family, on the other hand, were newly ar-rived in the late 1950s from Terre Haute, Indiana. Her father had taken a job in Fairmont, a stolid middle-class town on the Monongahela River, as the manager of a bottling plant. He was a meat-and-potatoes man. He and his wife didn't want to experience anything too rural or off-brand; they didn't want to be confused with mountain coots. He was a chain-smoker and wore dentures; they were the first I'd seen, and the fam-ily's food, as he aged, gave way to them. Meat was fork-tender. Meals aspired to the condition of pureed yams.

My parents met in the early 1960s when my father was in his final year at the West Virginia University College of Law and my mother was homecoming queen at Fairmont State University, a former teachers college. They married, moved to Charleston (the state capital), and had the three of us: me, then my sister, Anne, and then my brother, Bill. A few years later they fled with us to Naples, Florida. In 1973, we entered our first house, at night, during a flooding summer rain. Floating red ants in lily-pad formations clung to our legs and stung in unison, as if avenging an ancient mound desecration. *Welcome*, they seemed to say, *to the Sunshine State*.

I grew up on my mother's generous middle-class American cooking. I loved its warm-buttered-noodle blandness. Jane and Michael Stern, in their book *American Gourmet*, lift and separate, as the bra ads used to say, the culinary dividing lines of the 1960s and '70s, when I was a kid. "On one side were TV dinners, Wonder bread, Hamburger Helper, Cool Whip, and Richard Nixon in the White House eating his allegedly favorite snack of cottage cheese and ketchup," they wrote. On the other side, as I recall, were tahini, tamari, tofu, turmeric tea, Carole King albums, carob, batik dresses, and *Our Bodies, Ourselves*. Culturally and culinarily, we were on the Cool Whip side of this divide, even if Hamburger Helper was, for us, definitely infra dig. Still, about this era I can say: we all lived in a Jell-O submarine.

This might be the place to mention that my mother was more beautiful than other people's. Does every son think this? With her hazel eyes, button nose, and shoulder-length dark brown hair, she resembled an Appalachian Natalie Portman. She looked good in long white gloves; she was also excellent to have around in a crisis. She could rewire a fuse box, put up drywall, lay linoleum, sew clothes. She was never more beautiful than when wielding a hammer, with her fine concentrated brow and a penny nail poking from her mouth. You could bring her a wasp-stung finger, an algebra problem, a skinned knee, and she would blink away the pain. As a bonus, she was easy to find: wherever she went, a nimbus of blue cigarette smoke and a tall glass of watery iced coffee attended her.

She didn't love to cook; it wasn't her thing. She had a set of toothsome standards, prepared in faithful rotation: sauerkraut with sliced-up franks; spaghetti with fried ground hamburger and a sauce made from Hunt's canned tomatoes, served with a gleaming green shaker of Kraft grated Parmesan cheese. She made hard-shell tacos with ground beef and teeth-slit packages of spices, and an Americanized version of egg foo yong. We tease her about some of these dishes, but we loved them. I miss that egg foo yong so much that, occasionally, I try to emulate it at home. It's always a wreck. Like Ralph Kramden in *The Honeymooners*, which my father fell asleep in front of during reruns in the years before my parents divorced, we ate a lot of meat loaf.

Sometimes we had fresh fish, snapper or sheepshead or snook, caught by my mother's father after her parents retired in Florida. My mother terrorized us about the danger of fish bones, which can snuff you if lodged in the throat. You could end up like Sherwood Anderson, who died after he accidentally swallowed the toothpick in his martini. I retain a vestigial sense of unease in fish markets, which are otherwise my favorite places. In *Look Homeward, Angel*, Thomas Wolfe's hero, a ravenous eater, chokes on fish bones. It's hilarious because they barely slow him down. "Each time he would look up suddenly with a howl of agony and terror," Wolfe wrote, "groaning and crying out strongly while a half-dozen hands pounded violently on his back."

My mother had a second sense for when one of us was disappointed, picked-upon, disengaged, or had their ass handed to them on a sports field. On these days she'd make a melty, heartening dish she knew we'd appreciate. Marilynne Robinson, in *Home*, captured this motherly predilection. "After every calamity of any significance she would fill the atmosphere of the house with the smell of cinnamon rolls or brownies, or with chicken and dumplings, and it would mean, This house has a soul that loves us all, no matter what," Robinson wrote. "It would mean peace if they had fought and amnesty if they had been in trouble. It had meant, You can come down to dinner now, and no one will say a thing to bother you, unless you have forgotten to wash your hands."

Mothers and food: a subject for a double-wide shelf of books. In *The Joy Luck Club*, Amy Tan wrote that "Chinese mothers show they love their children, not through hugs and kisses but with stern offerings of steamed dumplings, duck's gizzards, and crab." Amanda Hesser says a good recipe should read like a letter from your mother. And sure enough, Hesser's recipes are great because they feel like a little conspiracy between her and the reader. Jonathan Gold wrote that sometimes what you really want isn't a chef's finicky cookbook but his or her mother's more authentic and forgiving and thus profound one. (He was talking about Paul Prudhomme.)

God love them, my parents' taste in music resembled their taste in food. One year they bought a new car, and pre-installed in the tape deck was an eight-track cassette called something like *The Sound of Stereo*. They never popped it out or turned it off. It played for three years straight. The cover versions—"Gentle on My Mind," by Ray Conniff and the Singers, "Fool on the Hill," by the Percy Faith orchestra— have ladled themselves, like Velveeta cheese sauce, into the back corners of my mind. Against my will I came to love these songs. For the rest of my life, in recompense, I've prized sparer sounds, agreeing with the poet August Kleinzahler that most country and blues singers are best early on, "when they still have a bit of manure on their shoes and haven't quite learned the knack of playing to the public."

Table manners meant a lot to my parents. My mother had learned them at home. My father picked his up at his WVU fraternity, which was strict, in the late 1950s, about such niceties. We learned to shift the fork between the left hand, when cutting, and the right, when eating. William Faulkner ate this way. "He would cut his meat, put his knife down, pick up his fork, pick up a piece of meat, put it in his mouth, put the fork back, pick up the knife, and cut another piece of meat," an observer wrote. The first time I noticed someone eating in the European manner, in which the fork remains in the left hand, tines directed downward, I recognized the economy and thus style of these manners.

I recall my first inkling that such things might matter. I was in my final year of high school; the late movie was *Charade*, the 1963 Stanley Donen film with Audrey Hepburn and Cary

Grant. Little did I know that *Charade* contains the loveliest eating scene in the history of film, though it lasts only a few moments. Hepburn and Grant are dining at night on a boat on the Seine, their crisp repartee echoing off the stone arches of the bridges they pass beneath. She's a widow threatened by men who are after her late husband's possibly stolen money; he's a charmer who may want her money, too. The movie slows to a crawl—it did for me, at any rate—as Hepburn delicately picks up her fork in her left hand, tines down, and her spoon in her right, curved gently upward, and begins to compose a salad from a serving dish. She flicks lettuce and charcuterie onto her salad plate with preternatural adroitness and ease. This, one thinks, is what the poetical use of cutlery looks like. Her posture and manners are almost heartbreaking to observe. They certainly break Grant's heart. Watching her, he finally utters what's been on his mind all along. "Hasn't it occurred to you," he says, "that I'm having a tough time keeping my hands off you?" She melts, and after a moment her cutlery crashes to the table. One kind of spell has been broken; another kind has been cast.

There's an impulse to informality in American manners; few of us want to be seen as too fussy. One observer recounted a meal with George Washington during which "at every interval of eating or drinking he played on the table with a fork or knife like a drumstick." Of course, bad manners are more fun to read about than good ones. "I'd listen to the little slurping noises she made as she sucked the liquid in, and I used to hate her for that as for the most heinous act," Tolstoy wrote in *The Kreutzer Sonata*. Søren Kierkegaard's nickname in his family was "Fork," bestowed after he was criticized for shoveling his food greedily at the table. In response, he announced: "I am a fork, and I will stick you." The critic R. P. Blackmur watched Edmund Wilson eat spaghetti and commented, "It was enough to make you lose your faith in human nature." According to Joyce Carol Oates, it's the most famous thing Blackmur ever said.

I've never had a Proustian madeleine moment, a profound bite that brought everything sweeping back to me, and I sometimes dislike reading about other people's because the revelations can seem forced. But I often have reason to recall three early experiences—petites madeleines of a sort—that gave me an inkling that better things were out there. I'll try to be brisk about them, as if this were an oyster-shucking contest. The first was on a fall afternoon in 1973, when I was eight; my father and I were driving home after a Miami Dolphins football game. We were in a part of the Everglades that was a vast scorched nowhere, with mangroves and saw grass on either side of the sun-bleached two-lane blacktop. It wasn't uncommon to come upon an alligator lazing across the middle of the road, blocking traffic in both directions. A crowd was milling outside a cypress-log frame hut with a thatched roof. Smelling woodsmoke, we turned off the Tamiami Trail and pulled in. This was the Pit, where I first tasted barbecue. I'd get to know the Pit well over the next decade, but this first stop really made an impression on me. The Pit's clientele seemed to have spilled from a Harry Crews novel: shirtless pot smokers, maximum lawmen, poachers as tanned as cigar wrappers, with Tyrolean hats and rattlesnake-skin headbands. There were a lot of bikers, and the scene was chaotic. Dudes whipped out their greasy dicks and peed in the palmettos.

While we were in line, a thudding arrest scene played out. The cops had corralled a man with a hawk nose. There was white spittle at the corners of his mouth, as if he were a mad dog. Years later, when I read Norman Mailer's *The Armies of the Night*, I realized the truth of Mailer's observation that "an arrest was carnal. Not sexual, carnal—of the meat, strangers took purchase of each other's meat." My father and I took our trays piled with spareribs and fries and pickle chips and found a place to sit on the outskirts of the madness. In his biography of Robert Stone, Madison Smartt Bell writes about how Neal Cassady, at one of Ken Kesey's parties, injected a pig destined for a barbecue with LSD. I can imagine a similar scene playing out at the Pit. I took my first bite of a sparerib and felt elation and fury creep over me at the same time: I *could not believe* ribs had been kept secret from me.

The second moment was in West Virginia, in Archie's kitchen in Mannington. He didn't drink, but he had a favorite nightcap. When peaches were in season, he'd slice one into a bowl and eat it at midnight after covering it with whole milk. One August night when I was young, we were the last ones up after listening to a Pirates game on the radio. I followed him into the kitchen, and he inducted me into his bedtime ritual. It remains one of my favorite things, an anchor for a bountiful night's sleep. Now it's one of my children's favorite things. Mary McCarthy, in *Memories of a Catholic Girlhood*, remembers her father teaching her how to eat a peach "by building a little white mountain of sugar and then dipping the peach into it." The method didn't matter as much, she intuited, as the way her father "insisted on turning everything into a treat."

My final sub-Proustian moment involves blue crab. My uncle Bill, my mother's brother, was a pilot with United Airlines. He and his wife, Robin, a former stewardess who was bronze of leg and brutal of wit, had a house in Maryland with a distant view of Chesapeake Bay. I was nine or ten and visiting with my family. Bill wrestled the crabs into a pot filled with boiling water and, not long after, dumped them out, red and steaming, onto a backyard picnic table covered with newspapers (reading!) and napkins and Old Bay seasoning. I was ensorcelled by the chaos of it: cracking shells with hammers, pulling meat from the interstices of claw, leg, and shell, blithely spattering shirts and shorts and shoes. We didn't eat this way at home. After this, one definition of a good meal, for me, became: *one after which the table must be hosed down*. Bill knew how to handle corn, too. He brought a second pot of water to boil and speed-walked out to his garden, as if striding on hot coals. He hacked a dozen ears of corn from their stalks with a machete and strode back, shucking on the run, preserving the natural sugars before they turned to starch, then plunged them into the pot for a fast steam. I absorbed Bill's unspoken lesson, which was: worship corn like an Aztec.

I recall, too, a reverse-Proustian moment. I had an afternoon newspaper route when I was eleven and twelve, delivering the *Naples Daily News*, which local wits referred to as the *Daily Mullet Wrapper*. One of the priests at Saint Ann offered to give me a slice of homemade apple cake anytime I brought him a free paper. I always had extras, so this seemed like a good deal. One afternoon, while I was in his apartment, he said he had to use the bathroom. He stood up in the living room and pulled down his pants and underpants. There it was, like an aspergillum, dangling between his legs. After a few seconds, he strolled away to the bathroom, calling out behind him, "Don't worry, we all have the same parts!" I shook the experience off, like a dog emerging from water. But I never went back, and I not entirely coincidentally became an atheist not long after. I have never since eaten apple cake with much gusto.

I was still in grade school when my weight began to be perceived as a problem; too many books and too many cheesy sandwiches. If I'd been a cat, my undercarriage would have swayed while I walked. I was ashamed of my plumpness, especially when I landed on the "skins" side during shirts-versus-skins basketball games. This was a dread, four-alarm situation, and there was no escaping it. My breasts bounced, and kids mimicked their heave-ho. Everyone else was thin and tall, like bottles of German wine. In seventh and eighth grade, I went to weekly Weight Watchers meetings in the church's fluorescent-lit rectory. I was the youngest person by two decades. The soft old ladies fussed and fussed over me. I remember eating, on my diets, a lot of canned tuna and fried calves' liver. I developed a craving for the latter. It's increasingly hard to find, a low- and high-status taste, most often found in diners or, conversely, on the retrograde menus at Manhattan's old-school social clubs, but seldom in between.

I've been thirty to sixty pounds overweight most of my life. I'm interested in fictional characters who share my experience. I'm attuned to the way fat men are feminized in Shakespeare. I know what Sigrid Nunez is speaking about, in her novel *What Are You Going Through*, when she describes some people as having "a slimness that almost certainly means going much of each day feeling hungry." I've managed to diet myself thin at times, and attempting to remain that way I've felt hollow at every moment. In Martin Amis's *Money*, the narrator says, "Unless I inform you otherwise, I'm always smoking another cigarette." Unless I inform you otherwise in this book, I'm always either starting a diet or flunking out of one, living and dying on a binge-starve cycle.

I tend to go on diets in which, like Jack Sprat, I eat no fat. My wife goes for the ones where you eat no lean. Between us, as the nursery rhyme has it, we lick the platter clean. High-fat diets puzzle me; they're like turning your car's wheels in the direction of the skid. I've often thought about attending a luxe reducing spa in the desert. I can't afford that, but I've unsuccessfully pitched a long series of editors on the idea. I fear I wouldn't have the fortitude. I'd be like my friend, the writer and editor Daniel Okrent, who spent only a few days at Rancho La Puerta—he calls it Rancho El Porco—in Baja California, before going over the wall for cheese enchiladas and beer in town, dragging another apostate along with him. Or like Mario Puzo, the author of *The Godfather*, who checked into a fat farm in the Swiss Alps. According to his pal Bruce Jay Friedman, Puzo couldn't hack it after a week, and he snuck out one night in his pajamas. He hailed a cab, somehow, and had the driver take him to Paris, three hundred miles away, for pizza.

My favorite poet may be the oversize Australian Les Murray, who died in 2019. I like a lot of things about him: his wit, his jumbo intellect, the essential wildness of his vision. I like his class politics, which speak to someone who is sometimes made to feel the cultural cringe of coming from West Virginia. In his *Paris Review* interview, Murray bragged that he'd "managed to wrestle life onto my terms without ever rising socially." He was large from birth; I like even more his poems about being stout. In "Burning Want," he recalled a childhood during which

> . . . *all my names were fat-names, at my new town*
> *school.*
> *Between classes, kids did erocide: destruction of sexual*
> *morale.*
> *Mass refusal of unasked love; that works. Boys cheered*
> *as seventeen-*
> *year-old girls came on to me, then ran back whinnying*
> *ridicule.*

In "On Home Beaches," he recalls being a fat kid at the shore. The line that kills me is the one in which he recalls being a "red boy, holding his wet T-shirt off his breasts."

I attended Naples High School, a public school. I edited the school newspaper, and I wrote the copy for the yearbook. I became adept at writing captions about what the sporty and well-adjusted kids were doing, a bedrock skill for any aspiring journalist. I founded a literary magazine. I became a pint-size troublemaker. The ACLU twice volunteered to defend me: once when I tried to get the word "fuck," as carved into a desk, into print in the literary magazine, and once when I criticized the high school's administration, in the newspaper, for being dour about life, though not in those words. Some of the teachers who stood up for me had their careers damaged for doing so. I could be pretentious. I'd walk through the halls carrying two fat novels and three books of poems along with my schoolbooks. *Look at me, I'm literary.* I look back and cringe.

By then I'd developed a sideline in writers who wrote about people who liked to tuck into life. From Robert B. Parker I moved on to Calvin Trillin, whose come-as-you-are food writing is collected in books with titles like *American Fried* and *Alice, Let's Eat.* I was lucky to have found Trillin when I was young, to have been bitten and stayed bitten by his work. He's earthy, and skeptical of pretension. He championed vernacular eats: clam bellies, fried dumplings, scrapple. I often find myself thinking, while holding a fork in a strange situation, "What would Trillin do?" I moved on to A. J. Liebling and Elizabeth David and M. F. K. Fisher and Jane and Michael Stern and the novels of Jim Harrison, whose heroes I hoped to emulate. Harrison's slapstick tough guys are gourmands who like game birds and truffles but are just as happy to find a can of Chef Boyardee ravioli, a delight recalled from childhood, in the cabinet. His characters have what he called "unmitigated cupidity," not for money but for life and experience. The biggest praise Harrison had for anyone was to remark, in *The Beast God Forgot to Invent*, "He's literally taking bites out of the sun, moon, and earth."

At Middlebury College, too, I edited the newspaper. I've heard there's a sign above the entrance to the University of Texas at Austin's newspaper office that reads, "This is where grade point averages come to die." There should have been one of those at Middlebury. By junior year I was stringing for *The Boston Globe* and *The New York Times*. By senior year I was writing theater reviews for the alternative weekly in Burlington, and book reviews for *The Village Voice*. I didn't attend a lot of classes. Nor did I eat well. I'd befriended the college's special collections librarian, Bob Buckeye, who had a piratical grin and turned me on to the novels of Eva Figes and the music of the Mekons. We played a lot of racquetball. One day he brought me, as a gift, a Styrofoam cup filled to the brim with frozen homemade pesto. I didn't know what pesto was, but for some reason I pretended I did. Later I tried to scrape some up with a spoon, as if it were sherbet. Yuck. The pesto rotted away in the back of the dorm refrigerator. It would be a while before I was ready for pesto.

I owe at least 60 percent of my education to the periodicals room at Middlebury's library. I worked the lonely-guy shifts at the counter (Saturday night, Sunday morning) that others didn't want. The warmly lit, high-ceilinged, shabby-genteel space was mostly empty then, and I had a lot of time on my hands. I'd slide through the long rows of periodicals and grab a copy of everything, returning each time with an autodidact's Dagwood-size pile. It was a golden age, maybe the last one for American magazines. *The New Republic*! I'd never seen a magazine where the next article just *began*, not waiting for a new page and a fresh layout. Michael Kinsley was the editor, and every page shone under his nearly Martian intelligence. *National Review* had Florence King's bossy columns. I scanned for James Wolcott's work in *Vanity Fair* with such enthusiasm—here was a writer who cooks on all four burners—that I made a beeline for the microfilm room, where I unearthed his earlier work in *Harper's Magazine* and *The Village Voice*. *Time* had the bullish art critic Robert Hughes; *Newsweek* had David Gates, not yet a novelist and newly divorced from Ann Beattie, throwing acerbic curveballs as a book critic. *Spy* was new and felt like it had arrived from a planet where irony was ozone. Even *Vogue* and *Elle* and *Harper's Bazaar* were packed with well-flossed commentary.

Pauline Kael was already a confirmed hero, and her movie reviews in *The New Yorker* would run to five thousand yea-saying words. My passion for pro sports was waning, but *Sports Illustrated* had Roy Blount Jr., Dan Jenkins, and Frank Deford, and was thus unskippable. *Esquire* was the stomping ground of lightly grizzled outsider-insiders like Joy Williams and Richard Ford and Tom McGuane, each anointed by the waters of some Montana trout stream of the soul. The articles in *New York* magazine were all glitter and squalor, and a mordant introduction to a city I hoped to know. I waded through every issue of *Mother Jones* and *In These Times* and *Utne Reader*, liking the muddy-shoed politics but mostly finding them too earnest. I read *The Atlantic*; *Texas Monthly*; *Interview*; *The New York Review of Books*; *The TLS*; *London Review of Books*; *Hungry Mind Review*, where I would have a column in the nineties; *The Economist*; *The Chronicle of Higher Education*; *The Boston Phoenix*, where I'd become a contributing editor; and *New England Monthly*, for which I started freelancing, writing about the onanistic artist Vito Acconci, who'd just put up a much-loathed boxlike installation on Middlebury's campus that freaked out the squirrels.

*Dissent* and *Commentary* were rehashing old feuds I'd become curious about. You couldn't read these magazines without recalling Woody Allen's crack that if you merged them, you'd get *Dysentery*. *Maclean's*, from Canada; what was that about? *Foreign Affairs* didn't take, either. But *The New Statesman* and *The Spectator*, from London, were favorites because the writers weren't pinned down by news hooks; they wrote about whatever they felt like, even if that meant their hemorrhoids. *Rolling Stone*'s record reviews still set listening agendas. And in *The New York Times*, Maureen Dowd's late-eighties coverage of the first Bush administration had so much elastic snap that I scanned for her byline every morning. She didn't sound like a Gray Lady.

No food was allowed at the library desk. If it had been, they might have had to wheel me out, like a refrigerator, on a hand truck. Holly Golightly, in Truman Capote's *Breakfast at Tiffany's*, reads magazines in this kind of quantity and with this type of ferocity when she's stuck in a hick town with Doc Golightly, scanning the gossip columns and trying to forget that her real name is Lulamae Barnes. (Later, Holly owns the entire Modern Library.) One summer I stayed on campus, and the mail room, unwilling to forward students' magazines, instead put them out on long tables every morning. It was an entire newsstand, free for the taking. Snapping them up, I was like one of those dogs in Instagram videos who have a hundred tennis balls dropped on them. Reading them all, with the proper supplies, I gained eight pounds in three months.

College cafeterias terrified me. I had a fear of filling my tray and turning around and finding stone faces. It's the panic of the kid on the playground beside the whirling roundabout, unable to climb on and fearful of being smacked by something in the process. I retain a phobia of entering populated rooms alone. I took a lot of my meals out at Rosie's, a restaurant on Route 7, where I ordered split-pea soup and well-griddled ham-and-cheese sandwiches. I could afford these meals because I worked all those shifts at the library, and because the college paid a stipend to the newspaper's editor. At Rosie's, the big-boned waitresses allowed me to hunker down. Possessed of a stack of books and magazines, I'd stay for two or three hours—until my booth was needed, or until the lights began to flicker on and off.

Frederick Exley's *A Fan's Notes* was already a favorite novel, perhaps because, like his narrator, I sensed I was destined to be, in certain ways, a spectator in life—a fan. As I eased into my booth at Rosie's, I'd recall the scene in which Exley's narrator buys a pile of newspapers and goes to his favorite diner "where, sliding into a booth, I ordered tomato juice and black coffee and began my weekly ritual." Here's the ritual: he would carefully remove his favorite bits—the sports, entertainment, book review, and magazine sections—as if filleting a fish. Then he would fling the news sections "into the seat opposite mine, where, for all of me, they could remain forever unread." This was essentially my newspaper-reading method, too.

I had started writing book reviews. What Exley's narrator had to say about them got to me. "There was a period when I had lived on book reviews, when I had basked and drawn sustenance from what I deemed the light of their intelligence, the beneficence of their charm," he says. "But something had gone sour. Over the years I had read too much, in dim-lighted railway stations, lying on the davenports of strangers' houses, in the bleak and dismal wards of insane asylums. That reading had forced the charm to relinquish itself. Now I found that reviews were not only bland but scarcely, if ever, relevant; and that all books, whether works of imagination or the blatant frauds of literary whores, were approached by the reviewer with the same crushing sobriety. I wanted the reviewer to be fair, kind, and funny. I wanted to be made to laugh. I had no better luck that Sunday than on any other." Like Exley's narrator, I like finding a good book review in the morning paper. That's part of why I kept writing them.

It took me a long time to graduate from Middlebury. I took a year off to bum around Europe. It didn't go well. I ran out of money and, not wanting to slink home in defeat, worked for three months in a pub outside London. I learned to make Scotch eggs and to like a warm pint tucked beside a ploughman's lunch. Anthony Bourdain was right about the mischief restaurant managers will get up to. At our manager's orders, we topped up bottles of white wine with water when they were a third empty. A few years later, still in college, I took a semester off to write a novel. That was a disaster, too. I moved back to Naples to live in a friend's unoccupied apartment. I wrote (poorly) during the day and, at night, worked the overnight shift at a last-chance Exxon gas station out on the edge of the Everglades. Almost no one came in after midnight, and I read novels while stuffing myself with Drake's Ring Dings, tubs of Cheez Balls, single-serving bags of Famous Amos cookies. I rarely, I am sorry to admit, rang these morsels up on the cash register. I remember reading a mass-market paperback collection of David Leavitt's short stories in that Exxon. He'd begun publishing, in William Shawn's *New Yorker*, the first overtly gay short stories to appear in the magazine. I'm not gay—alas, I sometimes think, because I'd fit right in with the bears. But, curious about the lives Leavitt was describing, and wondering how it all worked, I bought a copy of *The Joy of Gay Sex*, written by the novelist Edmund White with a doctor named Charles Silverstein, and read it at the counter. I'd tuck it away when customers came in, because in the mid-1980s you could take a punch for reading something like that in public.

I graduated from college in 1989. I didn't know where to go or what to do. How to make a career out of reading? I picked strawberries on a commercial farm for a summer and drove a big box truck, making deliveries for an organic sprout company. I was a fan of the radical journalist Raymond Mungo's witty memoirs, especially *Total Loss Farm*, about trying to make a go of it on a commune in Vermont. I thought about giving rural life a go. Instead, I moved to Burlington, the big city, and became a contributing writer and later an editor for an alternative weekly there. I worked for Burlington's indie bookstore, Chassman & Bem. Employees called it Chastise & Blame, because one of the owners was a scold. I shopped for food at the co-op because that's where the adorable hippie girls congregated. I was living on bagels and cheddar cheese and cereal and beans and trying to pay the rent.

I met Cree.

She was working for a community action group, helping hard-up people with their heating issues. She also waited tables at Sneakers, a restaurant known for its lavish eggs Benedict. The line cook at the time was Dan Chiasson, who would grow up to become poetry critic for *The New Yorker*. Sneakers was a hangout for the guys in Phish, a band on the verge of breaking out nationally. I didn't *get* Phish's music, and I said so in print. This was like criticizing Aretha Franklin in Detroit in 1961. I took a weeks-long beating in the letters column. By this time, I was itching to leave for New York, but I couldn't work up the nerve. I was like one of Chekhov's thwarted rural characters, the ones who keep muttering, "I must move to Moscow."

I'd begun to perceive, though she downplayed it, that Cree had grown up in a left-of-the-dial food family, and a serious one. Her father, Bruce, was a self-taught cook who'd run restaurants in Aspen and in rural Idaho and in the Napa Valley that were beloved by people who knew the real thing when they encountered it. Bruce had picked up his interest in food while in France working as an army counterintelligence officer. He became a chef in an era when it was blue-collar work, not something a Dartmouth graduate (as he almost was, having left one semester shy) would do. Bruce had hands the size of catcher's mitts and asbestos fingers that could snatch a nugget of meat from boiling stock. His food was, at heart, French rural cooking, farm-to-table before that phrase became a cliché. In most of his restaurants, guests got their table for the night; they could stay until 1:00 a.m. if they wanted. Many did.

Bruce had opened his first restaurant, the Paragon, in Aspen in 1965, after spending a thwarted year trying to write a novel. Cree's family's next-door neighbor in Woody Creek was Hunter S. Thompson, the gonzo journalist. He had just published *Hell's Angels*, his first book. Thompson was a regular dinner guest at Cree's house. During dinners outside in summer, he'd find a hose and spray the crowd down. Another regular guest was Oscar Zeta Acosta, the Chicano writer, lawyer, and activist who was the model for Thompson's "Dr. Gonzo." Acosta was a big man with jumbo-size appetites. After a big dinner, he'd thank Bruce for the "sandwiches." The *Times* food writer Craig Claiborne visited Aspen in 1969 and singled out the Paragon. He wrote, "It is possible that the most imaginative menus in America per capita can be found in this little town 200 miles from Denver."

When Cree was eight, her family moved to Idaho. Bruce opened a restaurant at Robinson Bar, a guest ranch with buildings that dated from the 1870s. It was in nowheresville, a ninety-minute drive from Ketchum on days when the roads weren't snowed in. The family raised nearly everything the restaurant served. They grew their own produce and made their own butter; they raised cows and Muscovy ducks; the eggs they cooked with were still warm from the hens. Then Cree's parents divorced. Bruce opened his last restaurant in St. Helena, California, in 1981. There, he kept a small army of foragers in business. One of these, a retired Chicago detective known only as Mrs. Herb, raised snails for him. The family I was marrying into was a long way from ham-and-cheese sandwiches, potato chips, and drinks made from powder. Cree grew up taking leftover frog legs to school in her lunch box. When I met her, she was in flight from her foodie past. She'd become a vegetarian and was eating the same sort of co-op meals I was. We took hold of each other's lapels and shook like hell; our appetites awakened.

I proposed marriage to her in Tallassee, Alabama, in a restaurant known for its fried chicken. When Cree got into graduate school at New York University in 1993, we scrammed to the city together. We had no money. I wrote a lot of essays and criticism for *The Boston Phoenix* and *The Village Voice* and sometimes *The Nation*. It was no way to make a living. Scared of being forced out of New York and sent back to Vermont, like a satellite that bounces off the earth's atmosphere, I took a job as a low-level features editor at *Harper's Bazaar*, edited by Liz Tilberis. The women at *Bazaar* wore black, had high foreheads, and were eleven feet tall. I wore corduroys and fuzzy shoes and had ill-kempt facial hair. I was the worst-dressed human, I was assured, to ever set foot in these hallowed offices. I left *Bazaar* to become the founding books editor of *Salon*, the first real online magazine, which debuted in 1995. Online magazine? I didn't have email yet. I feared no one would be reading, that I'd be throwing my writing down a hole. But *Salon* prospered. On the side, I was writing restaurant reviews for *Paper*, the downtown magazine, where I picked up a habit of ~~stealing~~ collecting restaurant ashtrays. I became an editor at *The New York Times Book Review* in 1998—what gods editors seemed then, when they were mysterious, before you could flick through their Instagrams—and I left editing to become a daily book critic for the *Times* in 2008.

You will sense me moving around in this book. Baudelaire, who lived at twenty-three different addresses in Paris, wrote about "the horror of settling down." He called it a disease. It's a horror we seem to share. Cree and I have spent a lot of time, on purpose, in transit. Our children, Penn and Harriet, were born in New York City, where we had a tiny apartment on Jane Street. The West Village was almost affordable then; our rent was $1,200 a month. The neighbor downstairs was a self-identified Satanist who liked to show off his collection of shiv-concealing umbrellas. He boiled and roasted beef bones all day. (I hope they were beef bones.) The unholy reek came up through the floor.

The one-bedroom Jane Street apartment was too small to contain our two squirming children so we moved to ex-urban Garrison, New York, where we stayed for a happy decade. Then, following friends, we left for Frenchtown, New Jersey, where we lived until Penn and Hattie were out of high school. Cree and I have lived since in Harlem; in Fairmont, West Virginia, where I was born; in New Orleans; and in Provincetown, Massachusetts. We're currently back in New York City, perhaps for good this time. We aren't rich folks who "divide our time."* We don't own even one house, an unforced financial error. We've simply found that we like being vaguely nomadic, slipping in and out of places, seeing America from canted angles. This too is observation greed. But it has meant that for several years our four hundred or so cookbooks have been in a storage locker. This hurts because, when off duty, reading cookbooks is how I unwind. I read myself to sleep with them, as did Jean Rhys, who wasn't a good cook but told interviewers she brought Marcel Boulestin's French cookbooks with her to bed. I go to bed thinking about what's for breakfast, and at breakfast I want to talk about what's for dinner. I live with someone who is mystified by this tendency.

In the kitchen, Cree and I are opposites. She's an instinctive cook who shuns recipes, even though one of her many cookbooks, *Fish*, was a finalist for a James Beard Award. I follow recipes to the letter and panic if I'm absent even the parsley. We're often at odds as eaters, too. She'll have the in-season fruit with yogurt; I'll take the three-cheese omelet with home fries. She has never, to the best of my knowledge, eaten in a food court or on an airplane because it wouldn't occur to her. Why not wait for something better? I smell the warm cookies in first class and can't wait for my little tub of indistinct protein—is that a belly-button-lint cutlet?—to arrive in 23D. She uses old hand towels; I go through paper ones. She has a bloodhound's nose for ersatz scent; I'll buy the perfumed trash bags and start using them without no-

---

* My favorite contributor's note appeared in the literary magazine *Raritan* in 2018. It read, "Gordon Lish divides his time between envy and resentment."

ticing. She can taste something and instantly break down its flavor components; I sometimes won't notice something tastes funky until I've nearly polished it off. Like her father, she invariably wants fresh things simply prepared. So do I, but I have a weakness for unusual ingredients and showstopping dishes—"stunt food," in her lingo. I recognize myself in dialogue from Gogol's *Dead Souls*: "When I eat pork at a meal, give me the *whole* pig; when mutton, the *whole* sheep; when goose, the *whole* of the bird."

Most of our fights are about food, although the real issues are as deep and layered as a casserole.* I envy Cree her childhood, in the way I envy people who grew up with books in their houses. She also had those in abundance. The only ones in mine were the Bible, *Reader's Digest* condensed books, and *The Guinness Book of World Records*, which Rachel Kushner called "a bible for the bookless under God." In other ways I had the better deal. People who grow up with too much good taste miss out. They don't get to make discoveries on their own. They don't have to work as hard for it.

Four decades after those afternoons on the living room floor, I still look for the food and the low-to-the-ground humanity in novels, as if to remind myself that, as Betty Fussell wrote, "the human animal is forever a bewildering compound of body parts and spirit sensors, a belcher of hymns, an angel that farts." It's a cliché but as valid as ever: when we talk about food, that's never all we're talking about. Food is a peephole into social class and ideological predilection; it's a

---

* Her least favorite food.

gateway to aesthetics; it touches us on instinctive, academic, mythic, associative, spiritual, and monetary levels. Like poetry, it offers clues to the beauty of living. It's as revealing as sex, and as we age, it's sexual compensation. As feeder and fed, we know the world by putting it in our mouths. Roth's hero Zuckerman says it: "Your mouth is who you are." Literary critics have long made crisscross tracks through food and its meanings. "Like the post-structuralist text," Terry Eagleton wrote, "food is endlessly interpretable, as gift, threat, poison, recompense, barter, seduction, solidarity, suffocation." Maud Ellmann calls food "the thesaurus of all moods and all sensations." For Roland Barthes, food is "a system of communication, a body of images, a protocol of usages, situations, and behavior." Gliding lower to the dirt, Jim Harrison wrote that "if you eat badly you are very probably living badly."

Unlike love, death, war, honor, and betrayal, food has not been among literature's great subjects. Many important novels hardly mention meals at all. Such domestic details were beneath the concern of male writers. Virginia Woolf, in *A Room of One's Own*, deplored this tendency. "It is part of the novelist's convention not to mention soup and salmon and ducklings," she wrote, "as if soup and salmon and ducklings were of no importance whatsoever." In her diaries, Patricia Highsmith apologizes to future readers for describing her meals. "Forgive food details, dear diary," she wrote, "but they become life details, perhaps." Appetite was once so seldom considered that Louis Untermeyer was moved to ask,

*Why has our poetry eschewed*
*The rapture and response of food?*

Orwell concurred, writing that "it is curious how seldom the all-importance of food is recognized." He thought there should be statues memorializing cooks instead of politicians and bishops. Consider this book a tribute—my own set of statuary—to those who have written with insight and feeling about food. It's a slim volume about what I've taken away from a lifetime of reading and eating, lessons both creaturely and philosophical.

There are other books that have approached food from the context of literature. Even in the best of these, I find the same scenes analyzed: Proust's cookies; the boeuf en daube in *To the Lighthouse*; the grilled mutton kidneys at breakfast that, in *Ulysses*, gave to Leopold Bloom's palate "a fine tang of faintly scented urine"; the lunch that takes up nearly three chapters of *Anna Karenina*. These scenes are well-known for a reason. But there's a wildness untouched. As a reader, I sometimes feel a bit like the starving woman in Studs Terkel's *Working* who asks the server in a soup line to dig down a bit deeper, to get some meat and potatoes from the bottom of the kettle.

A few elite experiences are described in this book, but so is my devotion to fried bologna sandwiches. The West Virginian and the Manhattanite in me are locked, like an ouroboros, in constant battle. Like you perhaps, I'm snobby about a million things, but I'm not snobby about a million other things. If you must set this book down, I invite you to do as the critic Cyril Connolly once did, and mark your place with a strip of streaky bacon.

# 1
# BREAKFAST

Perfect love is milk and honey, Captain Crunch, and you in the morning.

—**ELMORE LEONARD**, *Swag*
(paraphrasing the Eddie Rabbitt song)

It's early in the morning and early in this book. Let's have a cup of coffee. I was eleven when I forced myself to start drinking it every day, made from Folgers crystals, scalding hot, and nearly stiff with sugar. The men and women I admired in fiction—the dissidents and misfits, the cool customers—took it black, usually with a cigarette. Charles Bukowski: archetypal black-coffee man. Ditto Raymond Chandler, who in *The Long Goodbye* wrote, "I went out to the kitchen to make coffee—yards of coffee. Rich, strong, bitter, boiling hot, ruthless, depraved. The lifeblood of tired men." Balzac was said to consume fifty cups a day; his bladder should be in a museum. New York City needs a coffee shop that sells a specialty drink called the Kierkegaard. Søren Kierkegaard's method was to fill a cup with sugar until the mound rose above the rim. Then he'd pour strong black coffee on top, slowly dissolving the pyramid. Then he'd drink the devil-ready result. I made one of these once; it made me feel like a werewolf. M. F. K. Fisher told us that coffee is the *one thing* never to economize on. Maybe she's right, but food people say that whatever they're talking about—eggs, fish, oil, vanilla, yogurt—is the one thing to never cheap out on, so your shopping bill approaches the cost of a speeding ticket.

So many people are deathly serious about their caffeination. My beloved Cree, alas, is among them. She'll walk, and this is not hyperbole, three miles for a good flat white. I'm more equable. On some level I've never had a bad cup of coffee, in the same way I've never read a bad Lorrie Moore short story, though some are better than others. Ralph Ellison cared about getting his caffeination right. When he was teaching at Bard College in the early 1960s, he became roommates with Saul Bellow, who'd bought a decaying mansion nearby and was often lonely in it. Ellison enlightened Bellow about the charms of good coffee. Bellow wrote in his journal, "He had been taught by a chemist to do it with ordinary laboratory paper filters and water at room temperature. The coffee then was heated in a bain-marie—a pot within a pot. Never allowed to boil."

Cree is frequently anguished by sophisticated coffee equipment that fails to do its job. She's always making minute adjustments to the frother. It's probably true, as Christopher Sorrentino wrote in his novel *The Fugitives*, that people choose their espresso machines more carefully than they choose their lovers. If your machinery is basic, like the kind I prefer, you can try John Steinbeck's tip, included in his nonfiction book, *Travels with Charley*. To make coffee "shine," he wrote, drop an egg white and the shell into the bubbling coffee pot. Steinbeck's method was an old Swedish one: the egg white and shell are said to clarify the coffee, extracting bitterness and amplifying caffeine. Something in me would rather die than do this. Something in me would rather die, too, than drink coffee the way Laurie Colwin did. Colwin was a novelist who wrote two perceptive food books, *Home Cooking* and *More Home Cooking*. I like everything about them; I cook from my careworn copies all the time. Colwin's coffee habits make me shudder, though. "You can always tell if my sister and I have been around," she wrote, "because both of us collect all the dead coffee from everyone's morning cup, pour it over ice, and drink it." FFS, Laurie. Well, we all have our kinks. Richard Brautigan's kink was to put photographs of his girlfriends on the covers of his novels. You scan these covers and recall his comment, "The fact that she had large firm breasts and was a Democrat made her the perfect woman for me." He also wrote, in *Revenge of the Lawn*, that "sometimes life is merely a matter of coffee and whatever intimacy a cup of coffee affords."

A cup of coffee carves out a parenthesis in the day. If you can learn to shrink the hours between the morning's last cup and the evening's first drink, you've taken a baby step toward enlightenment. Frank O'Hara, in *Lunch Poems*, described making coffee on a desolate rainy morning, his hot plate "the sole heat on earth." O'Hara feared falling into nonentity; his coffee gave him momentary purchase, as if he were a radio powered by a little nine-volt battery. The undervalued novelist Charles Wright wrote about a similar rainy morning in his novel *The Wig*. He described making coffee that was "spiced with potents which would enable you to face The White Man come Monday morning."

I'm ashamed to admit I have a lucky coffee mug. It's from *The Guardian*, the London newspaper. I'm not sure how it came to be lucky, but I sip from it while on important deadlines, rubbing its belly as if it were a Buddha. A few thousand trips through the dishwasher have distressed it. I bark at my children when I catch them using it; they're toying with my karma. The best coffee mug I've come across in literature is brandished by a woman in Namwali Serpell's mighty novel *The Old Drift*. It reads: DECOLONISE YOUR PUSSY.

I've lived in Manhattan off and on, sometimes in apartments the size of a few Teslas. It's often simpler to go out for coffee. I like Ottessa Moshfegh's reasoning when she explains, in her novel *My Year of Rest and Relaxation*, why bodega coffee is preferable to Starbucks. At a bodega, she says, you don't have to "confront anyone ordering a brioche bun or no-foam latte. No children with runny noses or Swedish au pairs. No sterilized professionals, no people on dates." She adds, "The bodega coffee was working-class coffee—coffee for doormen and deliverymen and handymen and busboys and house-keepers." The man at the bodega will remember your name, and whether you want milk with that.

It's easy to take aim at Starbucks, that faux-wood-paneled purveyor of industrial premium-blend culture. In his novel *Antkind*, Charlie Kaufman's narrator really sticks in the knife. "Starbucks is the smart coffee for dumb people," he says. "It's the Christopher Nolan of coffee." In Starbucks' defense, I've been on road trips with my family in which the sight of one, after days of brackish truck stop coffee, made us bounce up and down in the car. Is Starbucks elitist? Bill O'Reilly, the disgraced former Fox News host, used to brag that he never went to Starbucks because he preferred a local Long Island coffee shop "where cops and firemen hang out." Michael Kinsley, in *Slate*, skewered O'Reilly's reverse snobbery. "Guess what,

Bill!" he wrote. "Cops and firemen like good coffee too! And they can afford it. Starbucks is one of the great democratizing institutions of our time. You'd know that if you went in there occasionally. You snob."

The snobbiest coffee in the world—the most expensive, at any rate—is kopi luwak, produced mainly in Indonesia. It is harvested from coffee cherries that have fermented in the intestines of a civet. I'd want Ralph Ellison's laboratory paper filters to strain it. It sells for six hundred dollars a pound. In Viet Thanh Nguyen's novel *The Committed*, coffee dealers handle this stuff as carefully as Meyer Lansky's crew must have handled the mafia kingpin's favorite dish, cheese blintzes. Kopi luwak sippers have nothing on Bennie Salazar, the musician turned producer in Jennifer Egan's ebullient novel *A Visit from the Goon Squad*. Bennie sprinkles gold flakes into his coffee because he's heard that they're an aphrodisiac. (They're not.)

I read and write in coffee shops, for an hour or two or three, most days. (Book critics live like grad students.) Magic things, in my experience, happen in them. Here's one example: When I lived in Garrison, I spent a lot of time in the Peekskill Coffee House, a fifteen-minute drive away. I liked it there because the place felt like a big shaggy living room. There was space for everyone. One afternoon in the late aughts, I brought along Hattie, who was in second or third grade. We were standing in line to place our order when I noticed an older man, behind me, staring at her intensely and beaming. The staring went on a beat too long. Who was this deviant? I gave him a raised-eyebrow look that said, "What?" He fumbled to introduce himself. He was Rob Shepperson, the children's book illustrator. A year earlier, he explained, he'd been here, in the Peekskill Coffee House, at a table, struggling to find the face for the heroine of a book he was illustrating. We'd been here that day, too. He'd been stymied until he saw Hattie. He'd surreptitiously made sketches of her. Hattie's face became that of Hope, the protagonist of *The Memory Bank*, with text by Carolyn Coman. If we'd not been in line with Rob on the day I mistook him for a creep, *we never would have known*. It's a soulful, intelligent book, filled with sketches based on my soulful, intelligent daughter. Rob, a lovely man, generously mailed us signed versions of some of his initial sketches.

\* \* \*

Increasingly I drink tea rather than coffee because it's easier on my nerves and stomach. When I do, I recall the advice in the only self-help book I've read twice: Tom Hodgkinson's *How to Be Idle*. Hodgkinson loathes coffee. He thinks it's for "guilt-ridden strivers, money obsessives and status-driven spiritually empty lunatics." Tea, on the other hand, to his mind, is "the ancient drink of poets, philosophers and meditators."

About tea, George Orwell is the essential voice, and his essay, "A Nice Cup of Tea," the definitive work. It's among the best things this vastly intelligent and earthy man wrote. Orwell began by noticing that, if you look up "tea" in a cookbook's index, it's rarely there. This is maddening because, he wrote, "tea is one of the mainstays of civilization." It's doubly maddening because "the best manner of making it is the subject of violent disputes." Orwell wrote his essay before tea bags had displaced the rituals of a well-made cup of loose-leaf tea,* but most of its principles still apply.

Orwell has eleven rules for good tea. Three really matter. The first is: make it strong. ("I maintain that one strong cup of tea is better than twenty weak ones.") The second: take the mug to the teapot and not the other way around. ("The water should be actually boiling at the moment of impact, which means that one should keep it on the flame while one pours.") The third: no sugar. ("How can you call yourself a true tea-lover if you destroy the flavour of your tea by putting sugar in it?") He advises, "Try drinking tea without sugar for, say, a fortnight and it is very unlikely that you will ever want to ruin your tea by sweetening it again." Contra Orwell, I do sometimes like honey in my tea. Writing is hard because thinking is hard, and when you're writing, a bit of sweetness can seem to inject you with that single extra IQ point you sense you need.

Christopher Hitchens picked up Orwell's argument more than half a century later. "Next time you are in a Starbucks or its equivalent and want some tea, don't be afraid to decline that hasty cup of hot water with added bag," he wrote in *Slate*. "It's *not* what you asked for. Insist on seeing the tea put in first, and on making sure that the water is boiling. If there are murmurs or sighs from behind you, take the opportunity to spread the word. And try it at home, with loose

---

* The lexicographer in Orwell would have been delighted to learn how much "tea bag," the noun, now differs from "tea bag," the verb.

tea and a strainer if you have the patience. Don't trouble to thank me. Happy New Year."

You could open a small bookstore stocked solely with volumes about the dismal history of the tea trade. Lydia R. Diamond, in her play *Stick Fly*, got at some of the reasons why. In *Stick Fly*, the LeVays, a well-to-do African American family, gather at their Martha's Vineyard home for a summer weekend. The dialogue is furious, even around the breakfast table.

> KIMBER: What do you think of Chai?
> TAYLOR: Highly overrated. I like the basics . . . Earl Grey, English Breakfast, Darjeeling . . .
> KIMBER: A fan of the colonialists are you . . .

In *Bright Lights, Big City*, Jay McInerney's narrator works at a magazine that resembles *The New Yorker*. "Generally," he writes, "people here speak as if they were weaned on Twinings English Breakfast Tea." I applied for an entry-level job at *The New Yorker* in the late 1980s. I almost got it, but in the end I didn't, in part because I couldn't (and still can't) touchtype. I suspect, too, that I came off as someone who knew fuck all about Twinings English Breakfast Tea.

In his memoir *Undertones of War*, the English poet Edmund Blunden recalled how much the rituals of afternoon tea, uniquely redolent of home, meant to soldiers in the trenches during World War I. The incongruity of a cup of tea amid the carnage of battle underscores awful moments in his book. "A young and cheerful lance-corporal of ours was making some tea as I passed one warm afternoon," Blunden wrote. "Wishing him a good tea, I went along three firebays; one shell dropped without warning behind me; I saw its smoke faint out, and I thought all was as lucky as it should be. Soon a cry from that place recalled me; the shell had burst all wrong. Its butting impression was black and stinking in the parados where three minutes ago the lance-corporal's mess-tin was bubbling over a little flame. For him, how could the gobbets of blackening flesh, the earth-wall sotted with blood, with flesh, the eye under the duckboard, the pulpy bone be the only answer?" The moment becomes still more appalling. Blunden continues, "At this moment, while we looked with dreadful fixity at so isolated a horror, the lance-corporal's brother came round the traverse." Blunden, who died in 1974, attributed his own survival to his diminutive stature, which made him "an inconspicuous target." In British fiction, tea's ubiquity makes it essential for scene-setting. When the host departs to prepare a pot, the narrator has time to sit alone, to catalog the surroundings, and to sharpen her insights.

When I don't use Assam tea bags, I use PG Tips, the venerable and inexpensive English brand, a blend of Kenyan, Ceylon, and Assam teas. They're come-as-you-are; no fancy tampon string and acid-tab paper are attached. Each tetrahedral bag resembles an oversize Snap 'n' Pop, those novelty fireworks that crackle when you smash them on the ground. PG Tips make me think of Van Morrison's "T.B. Sheets." It's a song about tuberculosis, a topic I don't want to mull while I make a mug of tea, but there you are. Wright, in his novel *The Messenger*, describes being too poor to afford food. As a stay against hunger, he'd put a great deal of cinnamon into his hot cup of tea, inhale the fumes, and consume the results in a determined gulp.

* * *

How seriously should we take breakfast, anyway? Perhaps seriously indeed: Lizzie Borden is said to have consumed a bad one on the morning she grabbed her axe. It's the least-analyzed meal, for sure. When Covid emerged and quarantine began, breakfast took on new meaning. Some of us were no longer grabbing coffee and a corn muffin from the mini-mart and hustling to work as if Vince Lombardi were chewing us out. We took time with it; we let it expand and fill more of the day.

With apologies to Marion Cunningham, who wrote a good one, and to Marie Simmons, whose *The Good Egg* is a whacking and not-uninteresting 464 pages, breakfast cookbooks are generally gratuitous. I've bought too many that I've rarely opened. The recipes you need to get through even a whacking morning are contained in books you should have anyway: *The Joy of Cooking*, Edna Lewis's *The Taste of Country Cooking*, and Amanda Hesser's *The Essential* New York Times *Cookbook*. If you need more recipes than this, it's possible that you (a) are the proprietor of a small café or (b) spend too much time thinking about breakfast.

We're defenseless in the morning, most of us. Slights are more wounding. At breakfast I like to have my family around me, at least three newspapers, and good bread for toast. The talking must commence *slowly*. Readers of the Harry Potter novels are routinely shocked at the way the Dursleys, the Muggle family, shun Harry at their breakfast table and later push bowls of canned soup into his room through the cat flap. We know Harry's met a friend when the half giant Hagrid invites him inside and cooks over his fire "six fat, juicy, slightly burnt sausages," which are not just delicious—they may be the first food ever offered to Harry out of generosity and fellow feeling.

There is a case to be made for breakfasting alone. Winston Churchill insisted on doing so, and credited it with saving his marriage. No one made the argument with more mongrel grace than Hunter S. Thompson, who injected the following paragraph into *The Great Shark Hunt*:

> I like to eat breakfast alone, and almost never before noon; anybody with a terminally jangled lifestyle needs at least one psychic anchor every 24 hours, and mine is breakfast. In Hong Kong, Dallas or at home—and regardless of whether or not I have been to bed—breakfast is a personal ritual that can only be properly observed alone, and in a spirit of genuine excess. The food factor should always be massive: four Bloody Marys, two grapefruits, a pot of coffee, Rangoon crepes, a half-pound of either sausage, bacon or corned beef hash with diced chilies, a Spanish omelette or eggs Benedict, a quart of milk, a chopped lemon for random seasoning, and something like a slice of key lime pie, two margaritas and six lines of the best cocaine for dessert . . . Right, and there

should also be two or three newspapers, all mail and messages, a telephone, a notebook for planning the next 24 hours, and at least one source of good music . . . All of which should be dealt with *outside*, in the warmth of a hot sun, and preferably stone naked.

Thompson was a self-mythologizer. It's wise to take his words, which lick up like flames, with a grain of salt. Thompson was following in the footsteps of Mark Twain, another imbiber of landslide American breakfasts. When he could get it, Twain ordered "a mighty porterhouse steak an inch and a half thick, hot and sputtering from the griddle," and that before the mushrooms and coffee and biscuits and buckwheat cakes. I like to imagine Churchill, Thompson, and Twain in Heaven, having at last put down their cutlery and toddling off for midmorning naps.

We like breakfast food because it returns us to the tastes and sensations of our toddlerdom, when we were most approved of by the world. "*Feed me* and *love me*," Diski wrote, "are virtually synonymous demands." Our mouths, when we are young, know what our minds do not. Who doesn't, as an adult, like to have breakfast for dinner? I'd have liked being a member of the dining club at Oxford in the 1920s in which the members regularly lived a day in reverse. In the morning, there was brandy and cigars in dinner jackets. Dinner was breakfast served by moonlight.*

---

* There should be more groups that meet over meals. In New York City I belong to the Organ Meat Society. We get together once a month or so to eat tripe and kidneys and blood sausage and sweetbreads and other delicacies, usually in the outer

*  *  *

I no longer keep cereal in my apartment because it has a certain power over me. I'll finish a box in a week, in furtive bowls consumed at midnight, with whole milk and maybe a dollop of raspberry jam on top. I'll be in my pajamas, leaning over the bowl, flipping through back issues of *New York* magazine. From behind, I resemble a bear that has knocked over a trash can. When I allow myself a bowl of cereal, I remember that Peter De Vries proposed, in his novel *The Glory of the Hummingbird*, that a thinking person's cereal might be branded "Joyce Carol Oates." I recall the moment in Donald Barthelme's witchy novel *Snow White* in which the characters regard each other around a breakfast table filled with cardboard boxes of "Fear," "Chix," and "Rats." In his memoir, *Little Failure*, Gary Shteyngart wrote: "Cereal is food, sort of. It tastes grainy, easy and light, with a hint of false fruitiness. It tastes the way America feels." Elif Batuman, in her novel *Either/Or*, is dead-on when she describes Cracklin' Oat Bran as "the most filling cereal, in almost a sinister way." William Faulkner added a "u" to his surname. If the estimable Batuman dropped the "u" from hers, her audience would triple overnight.

When I'm desperate for a bowl of cereal and none is in the house, my fallback is a bowl of Quaker Oats, eaten raw with whole milk and brown sugar. This is strictly bliss. Cree taught me this combination. Once, she caught me at it and

boroughs. I envy the club of classicists who meet twice a year at the Garrick Club in London to discuss a single Latin poem over dinner. They bravely call themselves the Flaccidae, or "Flaccids."

unkindly commented, "You know, that's what they feed pigs to fatten them up."

William Styron admired the big red "K" on boxes of Kellogg's Special K because they reminded him of Kafka's eponymous heroes, who go by that initial in *The Trial* and *The Castle*. The pop art painter James Rosenquist had a thing about Kellogg's, too. In his memoir, *Painting Below Zero*, he explained why one of his billboard-size canvases includes a red meteor crashing into abstractions of Kellogg's cornflakes boxes. "I have relatives who are farmers," Rosenquist wrote. "Inside a box of cereal there's about six cents' worth of grain, and the box, when you buy it in the store, costs $4 or $5."

I still like to read the backs of cereal boxes, although, increasingly, there's nothing there but some numbing graphics. Prose on food packaging should be well written. In the 1970s, a granola company called Absolutely Nuts printed Richard Wilbur's poem "A Wood" ("Air, water, earth and fire are to be blended, / But no one style, I think, is recommended.") on the back of its packaging. The mountain climber Eric Shipton noted that food labels used to be the only things climbers had to read at high altitude. Lewis Carroll's Alice reads a marmalade jar's label as she tumbles down the rabbit hole. This scene is a reminder, somehow, that the worst thing about death is that you can't take a book with you.

* * *

I cook two eggs almost every morning. The results often belong in the Hall of Fame. On gray days when I overcook them, they still belong in the Hall of Very Good. I confessed my daily egg habit in the *Times* and received several emails warning me of myocardial infarction. I have a hard time abstaining. So did Henry James, who wrote in *A Little Tour in France*, "I am ashamed to say how many of them I consumed." James Bond, in Ian Fleming's novels, eats scrambled eggs like a maniac. So well-known was Bond's penchant for eggs that a proofreader of Fleming's novel *Live and Let Die* noted "the security risk this posed to Bond, writing that whoever was following him need only walk into a restaurant and ask, 'Was there a man here eating scrambled eggs?'"

When we can, we buy eggs from the person who raised the chickens. I recall Gabriel García Márquez's experience in the 1960s, reporting in Cuba. Because Cuban housewives scorned mass-produced eggs with a "pharmacy taste," García Márquez wrote, savvy grocers would "daub them with chicken poop to sell them at a higher price." It's a sign of quality and serious- ness of intent to leave a smear of feces on eggs bound for market, the way it is to weave a bit of straw or sheep excre- ment into a wool sweater, or for a Mexican restaurant to have tripe on the menu. For a decade or so, while we raised our kids in a house on a dirt road in Garrison, about an hour north of Manhattan, we kept chickens in a coop out back. We fed them good kitchen scraps and the yolks were a hallucinatory sunset orange. All writers should keep chickens at least once. Striving to avoid cliché, they could appreciate where most of those in English come from. "Ruling the roost," "pecking order," "egging on," "henpecked," "fox in the henhouse," and other common- places become abstractions no more. The cliché "scratching out a living" is especially poignant when you are freelancing.

*  *  *

During the darker months of Covid, life was absent so many of the things that make it worth living—rock shows, theater, movies, dinner parties, candlepin bowling, and especially restaurants—that you learned to take your pleasures where you could. One hero in my house was Jacques Pépin, the French-born chef and cookbook writer. Shortly after lockdown began, Pépin, who is in his mideighties, began issuing short videos on Facebook that explained how to cook well using the homeliest ingredients. There he was, at a moment when going to the grocery store was frightening, making vegetable soup from odds and sods in the crisper drawer, nonchalantly cutting the dark bits from old vegetables. Making a choucroute garnie, he threw in sliced hot dogs. He made quick chicken breasts resemble an entrée that might have been served to Hemingway and Fitzgerald at the Café du Dôme. A French king of the tortilla pizza? He was.

With people out of work, and others fearful of joining them, and still others shell-shocked and instinctively practicing thrift, Pépin's recipes spoke to a moment. I found many of his videos to be, on certain insomniac nights, strangely and almost unbearably moving. His age, his battered good looks, his accent, the slight sibilance in his voice, his culinary erudition worn lightly, his finely honed knife skills, and the seventies-era funk of his wood-paneled kitchen: it was a mesmerizing package. I especially liked to watch him cook eggs. I'd study his method. Too often while cracking eggs, flakes of shell end up in the bowl. These are stupidly hard to fish out. To prevent this, Pépin teaches you to crack eggs *twice*, quickly, on a flat surface. This isn't foolproof, so I began to seek other counsel. In Bill Buford's book *Dirt*, about his time spent cooking in elite French restaurants, a chef warned him, "The egg: never cracked on the rim, only on a flat surface, once sharply, so as not to be contaminated by the shell, which is unhygienic." To recap: Pépin says twice on a flat surface; Buford, once.

Then on Hulu I caught *Big Night*, Stanley Tucci's movie about immigrant Italian brothers—chef Primo (Tony Shalhoub) and businessman Secondo (Tucci)—who open their dream restaurant in New Jersey. Primo's food is authentic, so much so that it's unfamiliar to the local clientele and their place is on the verge of closing. When word arrives that the bandleader Louis Prima is coming to eat, the brothers go all out. I've seen *Big Night*, a perfect movie, six or seven times. It ends with one of the most sublime scenes in American film. The morning after the disappointing night, Tucci's character wordlessly prepares an omelet in the restaurant's kitchen for his brother and another exhausted employee. Proof that life will go on, this omelet matters.* Tucci's method is impeccable. His face is as sensitive as that of Charlie Chaplin's tramp. You want whatever this beautiful man is making. Against the wisdom of Buford and Pépin, he cracks each egg on the *rim* of a bowl.

---

* A friend, the writer Max Watman, holds that there are two types of people in the world: those who come away from *Big Night* thinking about the labor-intensive timpano that Chef Primo makes, and those who come away thinking about the eggs.

Sylvia Plath, in a 1950 journal entry, written while she was in college, worried that being a wife would consist primarily of "cooking scrambled eggs for a man." She didn't want to become a mere manager in the domestic sphere. John Updike's novel *Rabbit Is Rich* suggests a reason why women might prefer to cook their own eggs. Updike wrote, "For their honeymoon breakfast he jerked off into the scrambled eggs and they ate his fried jism with the rest," a move I've heard described nowhere else, but maybe it's a thing. I sometimes use a calorie-counting app called "Lose It!" and I noticed when a woman commented on Twitter that you can log "sperm" on the app, at ten calories per serving. I had to look—and lo, there it was.

No writer has attended to mornings and their promise as closely as has Toni Morrison. For her characters, breakfast is sometimes the only bearable aspect of an unbearable day. There's a moment in *Song of Solomon* in which Ruth Foster Dead asks two boys if they'd like soft-boiled eggs. "You ought to try one," she says. "I know how to do them just right. I don't like my whites to move, you know. The yolk I want soft, but not runny. Want it like wet velvet." Ruth pumps water into the washbasin she uses for a saucepan. She slowly talks us through her method:

> Now, the water and the egg have to meet each other on
> a kind of equal standing. One can't get the upper hand
> over the other. So the temperature has to be the same
> for both. I knock the chill off the water first. Just the
> chill. I don't let it get warm because the egg is room
> temperature, you see. Now then, the real secret is right

here in the boiling. When the tiny bubbles come to the surface, when they as big as peas and just before they get big as marbles. Well, right then you take the pot off the fire. You don't just put the fire out; you take the pot off. Then you put a folded newspaper over the pot and do one small obligation. Like answering the door or emptying the bucket and bringing it in off the front porch. I generally go to the toilet. Not for a long stay, mind you. Just a short one. If you do that, you got yourself a perfect soft-boiled egg.

Whatever Morrison is writing about, you sense her turning it on a spit between the twin fires of her imagination. Ruth times her eggs by going to the toilet. Biological timing mechanisms of this sort aren't unheard of. The food writer Michael Ruhlman has a roast chicken recipe that basically says: put the chicken in the oven; go have sex; when you're done, so too will be the chicken. I once mentioned this recipe onstage, during a panel discussion. (I can't fathom what the context might have been.) The critic Daniel Mendelsohn stood up in the audience and dryly commented, "Whenever I try that, my chicken gets burned to a crisp." A final bit of egg wisdom, from Jim Harrison: If you're arguing with your spouse, don't chase each other around the kitchen island with cutlet bats. Harrison advised that it's therapeutic to go outside together and throw a few dozen raw eggs, hard, at a wall.

* * *

A few years ago, I caught a revival of Sam Shepard's play *True West* on Broadway, this one starring Ethan Hawke and

Paul Dano. I like productions of *True West*, in part because a lot of toast is flung around onstage, the way it used to be at midnight screenings of *The Rocky Horror Picture Show*. If you don't know Shepard's play, at one point a character goes on a nighttime rampage and steals all the toasters from local houses. "There's gonna be a general lack of toast in the neighborhood this morning," he says. Long ago I used to fear, when drinking, that I would do something like steal all the toasters in the neighborhood. Now I fear becoming the man in a different Shepard play, *Fool for Love*, who convinces himself he's married to Barbara Mandrell.

If *True West* is the Great American Toast Play, Nicholson Baker's first novel, *The Mezzanine*, is perhaps the Great American Toast Novel. Nearly everything Baker writes makes you want to hug yourself with happiness; his mind is like a helium balloon tethered to earth. Baker's narrator instructs readers to cut toast diagonally instead of straight across because "the corner of a triangularly cut slice gave you an ideal first bite." If you made the mistake of cutting your toast rectangularly, "you had to angle the shape into your mouth, as you angle a big dresser through a hall doorway."

I was surprised to read, in her *Essential* New York Times *Cookbook*, that Amanda Hesser doesn't own a toaster. Perhaps this is how she remains so enviably birdlike. Hesser argues, unconvincingly to me, that toasters take up too much space on the counter and that the oven does a better job. I use my toaster at least three times a day, and I wouldn't part with it. But Hesser is in good company. Samuel Beckett and Pearl Bailey sneered at toasters. "For bread to be toasted as it ought, through and through, it must be done on a mild steady flame," Beckett wrote in *More Pricks Than Kicks*. "Otherwise you only charred the outsides and left the pith as sodden as before." Bailey, in her book *Pearl's Kitchen*, wrote, "I still put butter on the bread and put it in the oven under the broiler . . . I guess I still have in the back of my mind the memories of people who did such a beautiful job of toasting bread on top of an old black wood stove." The problem is, she admits, she tends to burn it. When I was growing up, my mother ate the burned portion of any dish, reassuring us that she liked it best. In her memoir *In Love*, Amy Bloom reminds us to clean up our breakfast messes: "I leave the burnt toast in the toaster oven . . . I think, And this is how you get to Grey Gardens."

A friend, in college, exploited the fundamental innocence of toast in his romantic life. His move was to wait until it got late, when a party was fading out, and say to some girls he liked, with a mellow burst of apple-cheeked enthusiasm, "You know what I could really go for? *Cinnamon toast.*" It sounded cozy. The girls would muss his hair and follow him back to his room, where he kept a toaster.

\* \* \*

At home we sometimes splurge on fancy butter, but since we go through a pound a week we mostly use Land O'Lakes. In 2020 the brand removed the Native American woman from its logo. I'm down with that decision, though I mourn that generations of bored children will never discover the trick Lorrie Moore described in her novel *Who Will Run the Frog*

*Hospital?* Moore's characters devote themselves to "cutting out the Indian maiden from the package and bending the knees so that they appeared like breasts through a slot we made in her chest." The things we did for fun before the internet. We call our butter dish the "ditterbush," because that's the spoonerism that popped out of Penn's mouth when he was six or seven.

The English writer Henry Green, the author of the novels *Living*, *Loving*, and *Party Going*, said in his 1958 *Paris Review* interview that one of life's singular pleasures (he was paraphrasing someone else) is "lying in bed on a summer morning, with the window open, listening to the church bells, eating buttered toast with cunty fingers." Male writers love this line. They try to sneak it into publications that won't print the C-word. It's one of journalism's longest-running parlor games, watching them try to write around it.

\* \* \*

An easy and inexpensive way to feel beneficent is to cook a package of bacon (I use the oven method) before anyone else is awake. This makes you feel you've been handed, for no reason, a gold star on your homework. Sigrid Nunez, in her memoir *Sempre Susan*, wrote that Susan Sontag would sometimes cook a package of bacon and simply call it dinner. Bacon is the food of the angels, or at least of their temporal representatives. H. L. Mencken liked his soft-shell crabs with what he called a "jockstrap of bacon." My daughter will, without warning, become a vegetarian for months at a time.

Sometimes she'll convince a boyfriend to join her, thus transmitting what the lexicographer Jesse Sheidlower has termed a "sexually transmitted eating disorder." Bacon, sometimes, is what coaxes the ethically conflicted Harriet back to the other side of the fence.

In his *Life of Percy Bysshe Shelley*, Thomas Jefferson Hogg described Shelley's cultured vegetarianism at length. He wrote about the time he ate bacon in front of Shelley, who was disgusted. Shelley, curious, took a small bite and then cried, "Bring more bacon!" Hogg picks up the scene.

"Let us have another plate."

"I am very sorry, gentlemen," said the old woman, "but indeed I have no more in the house."

The Poet was angry at the disappointment, and rated her.

"What business has a woman to keep an inn, who has not enough bacon in the house for her guests? She ought to be killed."

I like ham as much as bacon with breakfast, especially country ham. I order packaged slices online because it's hard to find up north. Between the salt and the vacuum-sealed packaging, slices of country ham will keep in your refrigerator until well after the zombie apocalypse. In *The Taste of Country Cooking*, her classic cookbook, Edna Lewis wrote: "Ham held the same rating as the basic black dress. If you had a ham in the meat house any situation could be faced." This is Covid wisdom, and for any other time, too.

West Virginians are a biscuit-loving people. A Huntington-based chain, Tudor's Biscuit World, has a cultlike following. I eat biscuits with only moderate enthusiasm. They're so filling they prevent me from ingesting the other things I want to be eating. Like an unsolicited manuscript, a big biscuit can really punch a hole in your morning. I'd like to more resemble Ralph Ellison, who wrote to a friend in 1956 that he dismayed people "with the vast damage I could do to a pan of biscuits." Harry Crews, in his memoir *A Childhood*, wrote that he liked to puncture a biscuit and fill the hole with syrup, and then keep refilling the hole until it wouldn't absorb any more. He'd put two pieces of fried pork on top and share the plate with his dog. Crews is proof, if any is needed, that Southerners take biscuits more seriously than do other people. They're all over Eudora Welty's fiction. In her short story "Why I Live at the P.O.," Welty's narrator, a tough little nut, catches her uncle Rondo eating cold biscuits with ketchup in a negligee. In one of the great food-centric shards of dialogue in American literature, she asks: "Do you think it wise to disport with ketchup in Stella-Rondo's flesh-colored kimono?"

During the Depression, biscuits were used to polish shoes. The lard provided shine and helped soften the leather. Alice Walker has written about how, when she was young, she enjoyed "showing off my biscuit-polished patent-leather shoes." The narrator of Ocean Vuong's novel *On Earth We're Briefly Gorgeous* works at a Boston Market in Hartford where his hated boss has "nose pores so large, biscuit crumbs from his lunch would get lodged in them." I've always had sympathy for people with large nose pores—you will too, when you are older—and thus will never forget Tina Brown's description of older men "with noses like white strawberries."

Take the Chicago-born poet Patricia Smith's advice, in her poem "When the Burning Begins," for making corncakes in the morning. Take cornmeal and hot water and mix until sluggish, she writes,

> *then dollop in a sizzling skillet.*
> *When you smell the burning begin, flip it.*

Smith's instructions ("When you smell the burning begin, flip it") remind me of Norman Mailer's steak recipe, as related to me by a friend. It goes, and I am paraphrasing, "1. Fry in butter until the smoke alarm goes off. 2. Flip."

\*   \*   \*

There are foods I don't want to see in the morning. Claire Tomalin, a biographer of Thomas Hardy, wrote that his favorite breakfast was "kettle-broth": "chopped parsley, onions and bread cooked in hot water." In a diary entry from 1983, Richard Burton wrote about Elizabeth Taylor, "She stinks of garlic—who has garlic for breakfast?" Vladimir Nabokov was asked about moments from the past he wished had been captured on film. He replied: "Herman Melville at breakfast, feeding a sardine to his cat."

\*   \*   \*

Florida now has more shopping malls than a poppy head has seeds, but back in the early 1980s, when I was in high school, Naples had just one: Coastland. I worked in the record store, where we were forced to play the same five albums—the Go-Go's *Beauty and the Beat*, the Human League's *Dare*, Rush's *Moving Pictures*, Quincy Jones's *The Dude*, and Billy Squier's *Don't Say No*—so often that I know them as well as I would come to know the swirl of hair on the back of my children's infant heads. Whenever we could, we played scruffier stuff that corporate didn't allow. At parties at the manager's tiny, stucco-covered condo, we'd cram into the living room, the guys in skinny ties, and pogo to the double-heartbeat rhythms of "Private Idaho." I worked for both mall bookstores, too: Waldenbooks and B. Dalton. They were poorly stocked and run by managers who would never know the difference between Alice Walker and Walker Percy. But they were bookstores, and I maxed out my discount.

These stores had a few serious customers. From them I learned how to place "special orders" for the kinds of books we didn't stock, which was almost everything published before 1950. There's an emotional ghost-weight, I learned, that attends bookselling. People come to the register with their hearts in their hands, laying in front of you books about depression and cancer, loneliness and divorce, underachieving children and abusive spouses, or something sad and funny at the same time, like *The Diverticulitis Cookbook*. Ruth Rogers, who owns and runs London's River Café, has said restaurants are similar zones. We think of them as places we go to celebrate, but it's as common to have a customer learn, over their frisée aux lardons, they're being divorced or fired.

There are a lot of tears, Rogers said. On some nights, bookstore work took a toll on me. I felt I was sliding down along a corkscrew's spirals.

On my drive home, I'd pass the Dunkin' Donuts on U.S. 41, where my sister worked the evening shift. (Move the first "D" to the end of Dunkin', we knew, and it spells "Unkind Donuts.") The building was a glass box, brightly lit, a waterless aquarium. In the window, from a moving car, she looked like a figure from an Edward Hopper painting—a pharmacist of a sort, dispensing sugar and coffee to the plastered and the forsaken. I ate so many of the semi-stale leftovers she brought home in clear-lid boxes that, to this day, I can rarely bring myself to face a doughnut.

"If you really taste a doughnut, it's pretty disgusting," Ruth Reichl, the former *Times* restaurant critic, once said. "They taste of grease." The late British food writer A. A. Gill, who owned a slashing style, was an appalled admirer of Krispy Kremes. "The minute you bite one, you know it's the first of a chain that will last longer than your teeth," he wrote. "Americans don't buy them in ones or twos, they buy them in dozens in huge cardboard boxes and then eat them in solitary darkness."

I moped my way through my share of day-old doughnuts in solitary darkness. I was not a pariah in high school; I don't want to exaggerate, as memoirists tend to do, the extent to which I was an outsider. But I was inward facing, had a galaxy of pimples on my chin, and was certain I was, to borrow words from Chuck Berry in his *Autobiography*, "ugly as death eating a dirty doughnut." Long before Dunkin' and Krispy Kreme, doughnuts were well-known as consolation agents. There's a perfect moment in Edith Wharton's *Ethan Frome* in which the lonely Ethan, in love with the orphan Mattie, shares with her a meal of "fresh doughnuts" and "stewed blueberries." The Cambodian American protagonists of Anthony Veasna So's short story "Three Women of Chuck's Donuts" are a mother and her two young daughters who run an all-night doughnut stand in California's Central Valley. Like my sister in that Dunkin', they seem as lonely as lonely can be.

* * *

I read with envy in a *New Yorker* profile of the *Simpsons* writer John Swartzwelder that he works at a diner booth that he had installed in his kitchen. During Covid, I missed diners more than other restaurants, especially at breakfast. I enter and feel like Sal Paradise or Dean Moriarty in *On the Road*, searching for satori in a cup of java and a wedge of apple pie. Have you read *On the Road* recently? Early on, Sal and a hitchhiker named Eddie catch a ride through Nebraska with a cowboy in his truck. When the driver has a tire patched, Kerouac writes, in one of my favorite paragraphs in American literature, "Eddie and I sat down in a kind of homemade diner. I heard a great laugh, the greatest laugh in the world, and here came this rawhide oldtimer Nebraska farmer with a bunch of other boys into the diner; you could hear his raspy cries clear across the plains, across the whole gray world of them that day. Everybody else laughed with him. He didn't have a care in the world and had the hugest regard for everybody. I said to myself, Wham, listen to that man laugh. That's the West, here I am in the West."

I know that paragraph by heart because I have a framed copy of it, in a poster printed by Yale University Press, on my kitchen wall. Joyce Johnson wrote a dazzling memoir, *Minor Characters*, that's in part about her two-year relationship with Kerouac. They met on a blind date. Johnson recalls waiting for him in a Howard Johnson's, a diner of a sort, on Eighth Street in Manhattan. It was 1957, a freezing January night. He was thirty-four and struggling; the publication of *On the Road* was still nine months away. She was twenty-one and barely out of college. He was broke, and she bought him a meal.

"I've never bought a man dinner before," Johnson wrote. "It makes me feel very competent and womanly. He has frank-furters, home fries, and baked beans with Heinz ketchup on them. I keep stealing looks at him because he's beautiful. You're not supposed to say a man is beautiful, but he is. He catches me at it and grins, then mugs it up, putting on one goofy face after another; a whole succession of old-time ridiculous movie-comedian faces flashes before me until I'm laughing too at the absurdity of this blind date Allen has arranged. (The notion of Allen Ginsberg arranging blind dates will crack people up years later when they ask me how on earth I met Kerouac.)"

If you spend time in diners, like I do, it's hard to keep a nimble figure, what with all the fries, triple-decker sandwiches, and stale cake.* I sympathize with Pearl Bailey's mother in *Pearl's Kitchen*. When Pearl was growing up, she noticed that her mother never seemed to eat but was overweight anyway. Her children puzzled over this. One morning, Pearl's mother left something behind when she went shopping, and Pearl raced to bring it to her. As she passed the window of a diner, she stopped and gazed in. "There sat my wonderful Mama, pancakes stacked as high as her head, sausage on a plate next to them, and there were home-fried potatoes and coffee. Mama had her head buried down eating away." Her mother was ashamed and angry to be caught out while enjoying, not unlike Churchill and Thompson, one of her private pleasures.

Bailey doesn't talk about this in her book, but white-run diners were rarely welcoming places for Black men and women. In his poem "The Arkansas Testament," Derek Walcott writes about entering a segregated diner. He finds what he calls "my own area." He walks in and

> *A fork clicks*
> *on its plate; a cough's rifle shot*
> *shivers the chandeliered room.*
> *A bright arm shakes its manacles.*

Henry Louis Gates Jr., in his memoir *Colored People*, writes, "White people couldn't cook; everybody knew that. Which made it a puzzle why such an important part of the civil rights movement had to do with integrating restaurants

---

* I love stale cake.

and lunch counters." In 1961 Jessica Mitford got a look at a slick illustrated pamphlet called "Howard Johnson's Means People Serving People." About it, she wrote to her husband, "A glance at the myriad photographs reveals that it really means, white gentiles serving white gentiles." A waitress at a Southern lunch counter once told the comedian Dick Gregory that they didn't serve colored people. Gregory replied: "I don't eat colored people. Just bring me a whole fried chicken."

Diners—sometimes called lunch counters, or cafeterias, or drugstores—are all over the place in Cormac McCarthy's fiction. They're homes away from home for Cornelius Suttree, the protagonist of his eponymous novel. Suttree has rejected his parents' wealth and lives alone on a houseboat, earning money by selling the catfish he's caught. At the Sanitary Lunch, he watches a cook named Jimmy the Greek spear boiling meat from pots while "the fans that hung from the stamped tin ceiling labored in a backwash of smoke and steam." He wanders into a bus station café, while mourning the death of his son, and consumes "two scrambled with ham and coffee," which are served "on an oblong platter of gray crockery" as the cook turns "rashers of brains at the grill." Now there's a phrase—"brains at the grill"—that gourmands don't hear often enough anymore.

It's worth pausing for a moment to talk about food in McCarthy's novels. In real life, the writer has long presented himself as a man of simple appetites. When Richard B. Woodward caught up with him in 1992, for a rare profile that ran in *The New York Times Magazine*, McCarthy was living an austere life in a cottage behind a shopping center in El Paso and eating his meals off a hot plate or in diners. That sounded about right—in his novels, hash houses are timeless waystations. Meals there are, in this writer's hands, private acts in public spaces.

The existential cowboys in McCarthy's Border Trilogy novels, which are set out on the frontier, consume many of their meals fireside. But in *All the Pretty Horses*, the first novel in the trilogy, Lacey Rawlins peppers his eggs in a café until they're black. The proprietor comments, "There's a man likes eggs with his pepper." James Agee's novel *A Death in the Family*, which was regarded as the great Knoxville novel until *Suttree* arrived to challenge it, has a moving scene in which a woman remembers, on a dire morning, that her husband likes his eggs heavily peppered. I've often wondered if McCarthy was writing in homage.

McCarthy likes to feed his characters, and the food in his fiction resonates more than it does in most novelists' work. In part, this is because nearly all the lives in McCarthy's world are lived close to the bone, often in isolation, and food is a rare respite from intricate forms of pain. It resonates also because of the many violent and grisly sequences in his fiction: the baby, born of incest, left to die in the woods in *Outer Dark*; the rape of a woman's corpse in *Child of God*; the scalpings and other gore in *Blood Meridian*; the pneumatic cattle-gun killings in *No Country for Old Men*. It's a commonplace to say that food is consolation, but sometimes in McCarthy's work, food is a vivid reminder that we're all linked in the meat-wheel of life.

The reminder isn't always a welcome one. Take the macabre scene in his post-apocalyptic novel *The Road*, in which people are kept for food, a limb at a time, in a basement. They shriek for help. This tableau inspired one of the funniest pieces of wildcat food criticism I've ever read. The essay, by Helen Craig, was titled "A Meat Processing Professional Reviews Cormac McCarthy's *The Road*." It ran in 2014 on a website called *The Toast*. Craig pointed out that such a "living larder" is wasteful. Every day they're alive, she wrote, "these people will be depreciating in calorific value." Craig suggested, as any good butcher would, that "the ribs will be good fresh, and a pickling and brining process for the thighs and haunches should result in a product that is similar to ham."

Nothing in McCarthy's previous novels, however, can have prepared his readers—the hungry ones, at any rate—for the banquet of culinary observation in his recent book *The Passenger*, one of the two new novels he issued in the fall of 2022. *The Passenger* is more in touch with physical pleasure than anything McCarthy has written, as if he is eulogizing sensory experience itself. *The Passenger* is about a lot of things: salvage diving, incest, the nuclear bomb, lost cats, paranoia, and the higher realms of mathematics. It also happens to be about a nifty guy in his late thirties, a McCarthy stand-in, who drifts around New Orleans in the early 1980s and samples its delights. What's the use of a great city having temptations, as P. G. Wodehouse put it in *My Man Jeeves*, if people don't sometimes yield to them?

I lived in New Orleans for a period, and McCarthy brought the city back to me. His protagonist, Bobby Western, spends a lot of time in its bars, including the Old Absinthe House and the now-defunct Seven Seas. He reads his newspapers and takes his coffee, presumably with chicory, at Café Du Monde. He eats at old-school fine dining establishments such as Galatoire's and Arnaud's, but unless someone else is paying, he generally measures out his life in hamburgers, red beans and rice, and pie and coffee. He emphasizes the importance of filthy kitchens. "You cant get a decent cheeseburger in a clean restaurant," he says. "Once they start sweeping the floor and washing the dishes with soap it's pretty much over." The best burger Bobby ever had was at a pool hall in Knoxville. He couldn't get the grease off his fingers with gasoline.

One night at Mosca's, a throwback Italian restaurant outside New Orleans, Bobby and a private detective consume a couple of Sazeracs and then a platter of chicken a la grande, the restaurant's signature dish—pan fried, bathed in garlic and oil and herbs. Reading McCarthy on it was, for me, a Proustian arrow through my pan-fried heart. Chicken a la grande moves certain visitors to tears of gratitude. On another evening, Bobby and the detective have fettuccine with clams. The detective explains that you can't make food this intense at home because your stock will never be as good. "Unless you have an old rancid stockpot that you can just sort of throw every horrible thing into—rotten turnips, dead cats, whatever—and let it simmer for about a month—you're at a real disadvantage."

This scene charmed but puzzled. Brett Anderson, a *Times* food writer who lives in New Orleans and is an expert on that city's cuisine, told me that Mosca's has never served fettuccine with clams and wouldn't because clams aren't common in New Orleans's waters. Lisa Mosca, the restaurant's co-owner, said when I asked her, "It's possible that my aunt Mary would have made it for a special guest, but it's never been on the menu." So it sometimes goes in McCarthy's universe. He goes to great lengths to get details right, then throws his readers a curveball. After all, it's fiction. Asked about the fettuccine through his publisher (because how could I not?), McCarthy responded, in pure Bobby Western fashion, "No goddamn clams! Put a note at the bottom of the page!"

Bobby dislikes waste. At one point he drives past a dead doe on a rural highway in the wake of a wildfire, and he pulls over. The tone is Hemingway by way of Jim Harrison—he makes the meal nearly sound like an "experiential" dish that a restaurant like Noma would attempt:

> He got out and walked back with his knife and stood over the animal and made a cut down the charred hide of her back and laid open the tenderloin. The backstraps, the old hunters called them. He sat on the tailgate and ate the meat with salt and pepper out of small paper packets from a drive-in. It was still warm. Tender and red in the center and lightly smoked. He sliced it and ate it off a paper plate with his knife and surveyed the country where it lay in ashes about him.

Bobby enjoys the company of people who know what they're talking about, in any area of life. The wine talk in *The Passenger* is comically adept. During a lunch of snapper at

Arnaud's, an old friend from Knoxville orders a bottle of German Riesling because it's a bit sweeter than French whites, "which can double as window cleaner." When the bottle arrives, I mentally applauded as the friend waves the waiter away and fills their glasses himself. "Important to establish the ground rules at the onset," he says. "Excuse me. Don't even think about pouring wine into our fucking glasses." The sound *The Passenger* imparts is that of an old master making mischief. McCarthy's characters, for sure, know how to end an evening. Bobby asks a man what's in his glass and he replies that it's Fernet-Branca, the intangibly swampy spirit some think should be your last drink of the night because it's said to settle the stomach. The man says it for the rest of us: "Anything that tastes like this has got to be good for you."

But back to breakfast. Some mornings I do overdo it on the eggs, or the pancakes, or the biscuits, and I just climb back into bed. I've committed what the backgammon app on my phone calls a "casual blunder." Back under the duvet, I sympathize with the speaker in Joyce's *Finnegans Wake* who said, "I've eaten a griddle."

# 2

# LUNCH

Ask not what you can do for your country. Ask what's for lunch.

—ORSON WELLES

The idea of a long and generous lunch, with wine and gossip and more than a single course, plants a fissure in the post-Puritan American psyche. Who doesn't like the *idea* of a leisurely meal at midday, of one, two, or even three hours? We rarely permit ourselves the pleasure. We're strivers, most of us, unflagging, hardwired to grab something—a tossed salad in a compostable bowl, a paper cup of soup—and eat it, if not literally on the run, then at our desks, or behind the wheel, and get on with things. Norman Mailer, in a 1955 diary entry, spoke for most Americans when he wrote, "How I hated giving up time for lunch. So many ideas I had while I bolted my food, and so many of them must be lost." Gordon Gekko, in Oliver Stone's *Wall Street*, compressed the American sensibility into four syllables: "Lunch is for wimps."

The lunch canceler—*desertor prandi*—is a well-known species in Manhattan. When a plan for a proper restaurant lunch is made, it's usually nixed. On the morning of, a game of chicken begins: who'll lose status by canceling first? Even nonjournalists now complain of being perpetually "on deadline." In his poem "Barbara Epstein," Frederick Seidel recalled his friend, the late *New York Review of Books* editor, and remarked that she

*Could be relied on to cancel*
*The lunch date with you she herself had made.*
*It was her* tic nerveux *to have to.*

France and Brazil are among the countries where long mid-day meals are observed. But the great literary paeans to lunch, in my experience, come from England. The novelist Keith Waterhouse's primer *The Theory and Practice of Lunch* is especially recommended. It's a stylish hymn to midday decadence; a copy belongs in your back pocket. "Lunch is a celebration, like Easter after the winter," Waterhouse writes. He grows even more enthusiastic: "It is a conspiracy. It is a holiday. It is a euphoria made tangible, serendipity given form. Lunch at its lunchiest is the nearest it is possible to get to sheer bliss while remaining vertical." There's something slightly illicit about it, he suggests. One doesn't take one's spouse to lunch. We're playing truant; we're opting out.

Waterhouse has tests that a good lunch spot must pass. His might not be yours. His go-to salad, for example, is "thinly-sliced tomato with oil and lemon, nothing else." This he finds "remarkably difficult to come by." He won't return to a restaurant that's stingy with the lemons. "If a restaurant is mean with its lemons, it is going to be mean with every-thing." Well-made martinis are a plus. "I wonder if any mo-ment surpasses that of the second martini at lunch," Patricia Highsmith wrote in her diaries, "when the waiters are at-tentive, when all life, the future, the world seems good and gilded." The narrator of the English poet Christopher Reid's book-length poem *The Song of Lunch* makes the following noontime sighting:

*And there goes T. S. Eliot,*
*bound for his first martini of the day.*
*With his gig-lamps and his immaculate sheen,*
*he eases past you like a limousine:*
*a powerful American model.*

A bottle of wine should be ordered, not glasses. "Part of the companionship of being lunch companions is that you should take your wine from the same bottle," Waterhouse wrote. "It is, to be fanciful, as symbolic as breaking bread." The bottle should remain on the table, never allowed to be placed out of reach in an ice bucket. A good lunch is an event in the life of our morale. What you want to do is eat with a friend who will revel in your gossip, and cap it with their own.

*   *   *

I knew Waterhouse was my sort of lunch companion when he took up a special annoyance of mine: waiters who whisk things off as if paid by the crumb. Near the end of your meal, he writes, "If the cloth does not look as lived in as Spencer Tracy's face, then the lunch has been a failure. It should bear the honourable scars of battle—wine stains, soup stains, olive oil stains, spilled coffee, cigar burns—and be strewn with campaign debris in the way of bread crumbs, spilled salt, wine corks, toothpicks, sugar cubes, chocolate mint wrappers, cigarette packets and what have you." Here Waterhouse is in league with Shirley Hazzard, who described a table after lunch as resembling "a beach from which the tide had ebbed," and with Sally Mann, in her memoir *Hold Still*, who wrote about a meal with the painter Cy Twombly after which there was a "newspaper-covered table nacreous with oyster shells."

"The waiter who obliterates this impressive detritus is as a vandal wrecking the Albert Memorial," Waterhouse wrote. That paragraph should be posted in restaurant kitchens, above the photograph of the current *Times* restaurant critic. It's a rule that holds in bars—especially dive bars. If you've been at a table for a few hours with friends, it's gratifying to see the empties arranged around you like a crenellated embattlement. Your space feels occupied; better, you know what you've consumed.

A second English lunch-hour hero is Tom Hodgkinson. In *How to Be Idle*, he writes that the midday meal is "an occasion to be deliberated over, shared with friends and colleagues, savoured, taken over two or three hours." When Clive James became a television critic in the 1970s, before there were VCRs, friends asked him if he didn't mind not being able to go out at night. He replied, like the committed lunch man he was, "I hear all the good conversation I need when lunching on a Friday with drunken literary acquaintances in scruffy restaurants. In London, the early afternoon is the time for wit's free play. At night, it chokes in its collar."

\* \* \*

Friedrich Nietzsche liked a generous lunch. He foresaw that the meal was under attack by Americans. "The breathless haste with which they work is already beginning to infect the old Europe," he wrote, as if shivering at the thought. "One thinks with a watch in one's hand, even as one eats one's mid-day meal while reading the latest news of the stock-market; one lives as if one always 'might miss out on something.'"

Americans try to have real lunches. Thus S. J. Perelman in a letter to a friend in 1956: "Let's have one of those all-afternoon dialogues over much too much brandy, with nobody giving a damn but the waiter." There's no indication this assignation took place. In the publishing world, business was still done at lunch until recently. Reid's poem *The Song of Lunch* is about an editor who returns to an old lunchtime haunt, one he hadn't been to in years,

> *Not since the publishing trade,*
> *once the province of swashbucklers and buccaneers,*
> *was waylaid by suits and calculators,*
> *and a strict afternoon*
> *curfew imposed.*
>
> *Farewell to long lunches*
> *and other boozy pursuits!*
> *Hail to the new age*
> *of the desk potato.*

In his memoir, *Eating*, the editor and publisher Jason Epstein recalls the time Pete Hamill took Jacqueline Onassis, then an editor at Doubleday, to lunch in Manhattan in the 1980s. It was, Hamill commented, "like taking King Kong to the beach."

\*   \*   \*

A big lunch, in the sort of place where the forks are heavy and the plates light, can be alienatingly expensive. When I was young in Manhattan and on a limited budget, I approximated the leisurely ambience of a proper lunch by sneaking with a friend into a midday movie, ideally an action film or a comedy—something tangy, a Bloody Mary of a film. We'd hide in the cool public dark, eating popcorn and drinking soda. I still steal out, at least once a month, for a noon movie. "Guilt," as James Dickey wrote, "is magical."

I can't recommend a lunch of popcorn, although Ignatius J. Reilly, the autodidact, gas-emitting hero of John Kennedy Toole's *A Confederacy of Dunces*, made a meal of the stuff: he put away at least three big bags per movie. Stephen King likes to sit in a movie, he's written, with what he affectionately terms a "heavy bag"—one so loaded with butter that you feel you're carrying a wet kitten in a sack. J. D. Salinger, that nut, sprinkled dark tamari soy sauce on his popcorn. Mahalia Jackson, in *Mahalia Jackson Cooks Soul*, remarks that a little water sprinkled over the popcorn before it's popped makes it flakier.

One of the best things we did with our kids, when they were small, was to have what we called Popcorn Reading Parties. This was eating and reading for beginners. The rules were simple: make a big bowl of popcorn, grab a tall pile of picture books, climb into bed or onto the couch, and snuggle up and read aloud until the popcorn runs out—longer, usually. We sometimes got up to pop a second batch. Two of the books our kids liked best were food-driven: Rosemary Wells's *Yoko*, about a kitten who is teased for the "yucky" sushi she brings to school for lunch, and *Bread and Jam for Frances*, Russell Hoban's classic about a little badger who won't eat anything—not veal cutlets, not soft-boiled eggs, not chicken salad sandwiches—except bread and jam. Frances's mother serves Frances nothing but bread and jam, three meals a day, until she cries, "What I am / is sick of Jam." Before long, Frances is an omnivore; she tucks in like a champion. Popcorn Reading Parties worked for all of us. Books and Butter: an alternative title for the book you are holding.

*   *   *

H. L. Mencken didn't take a position on popcorn, but he blamed hot dogs for killing the American lunch. Once upon a time, he wrote, working people gathered in lunchrooms and packed away hearty local delicacies: "The chicken *à la Maryland*, the planked shad, the Maryland beaten biscuit, the steamed hard crabs, the jowl and sprouts, the soft crabs." Now we'd become herdlike, consigned to the cheap and the second-rate. If hot dogs *must* be eaten, Mencken wrote, let's raise standards. "There should be dogs for all appetites, all tastes, all occasions," he argued. "They should come in rolls of every imaginable kind and accompanied by every sort of relish from Worcestershire sauce to chutney . . . The hot dog should be elevated to the level of an art form." Mencken thought America should abandon the common weenie in favor of German-style sausages, which "run in size from little fellows so small and pale and fragile that it seems a crime to eat them to vast and formidable pieces that look like shells for heavy artillery." He saw all this sixty years ago.

Hot dogs raise suspicions. In *Portnoy's Complaint*, Philip Roth gets comic mileage out of a Jewish mother's fears about what her son is eating. She's worried about *both* of his primary orifices. "Alex, I don't want you to flush the toilet," Mrs. Portnoy says. "I want to see what you've done in there." She adds: "You go to Harold's Hot Dog and *Chazerai* Palace after school and you eat French fries with Melvin Weiner. Don't you? Don't lie to me either. Do you or do you not stuff yourself with French fries and ketchup on Hawthorne Avenue after school?" In a later novel, *Nemesis*, Roth repurposes this motherly paranoia. A boy has died from polio, and on the drive to the funeral everyone in the car is silent. As they pass Syd's hot dog joint, an aunt cries out, "Why did he have to eat in that filthy hole? . . . He wanted to be another Louis Pasteur . . . Instead . . . he had to go to eat in a place *crawling* with germs."

Before I left for college, I spent three months hitchhiking, doing a pentagram-shaped tour of the eastern half of America, from Florida to Indiana and then down into the American South and back up into West Virginia. Along the way I dropped in on a friend at a college in the South. I was startled to find him thin, pale, and in a fetal position. He'd been turned down by a fraternity of which he was a legacy and, wrecked, was dropping out of school. I thought a week of hitching—he'd never done it—would be curative. ("When in sorrow, learn something new," Richard Burton wrote in his diaries, quoting T. H. White.) I persuaded him to tag along. On our second night we were picked up by a big happy construction-working weirdo with outstanding eyebrows who listened to

Black Oak Arkansas cassettes and kept a case of beer in a back seat cooler. In the cooler, too, was a thirty-six-pack of Oscar Mayer (I think) hot dogs. Every so often he'd reach back, fish one out, and stuff it into his mouth. "Ya want one?" he'd ask, holding it in my face. We declined three or four times. "I ain't stopping until you both eat a hot dog," he said. It wasn't clear if he was joking, so we each took one. They weren't bad— not much different, at any rate, from the Vienna sausages my parents would put out at cocktail parties. Hot dogs became the unwished-for theme of this leg of hitchhiking. So often they were our only option. We laughed crazily in a Virginia diner, at the end of the trip, where the breakfast special was scrambled eggs with sliced hot dogs. Of course, we ordered them. The wieners, a bit charred, were heavenly.

Writers have spoken up for the humble hot dog. When Audre Lorde was a child, she wrote in her memoir, *Zami*, she'd nip money from her father's pocket to buy them. David Sedaris describes, in *Me Talk Pretty One Day*, a pretentious SoHo meal during which he longed for one. He goes outside, finds a vendor, and bliss. He's handed something "so simple and timeless that I can recognize it, immediately, as food." Nicholson Baker and Denis Johnson, in their fiction, have supplied ecstatic tasting notes. In *The Mezzanine*, Baker's narrator reports, "I ate a vendor's hot dog with sauerkraut (a combination whose tastiness still makes me tremble)." In the title story of *The Largesse of the Sea Maiden*, Johnson's narrator buys what he calls two "rat-dogs with everything." His surprise discovery: "They were wonderful. I nearly ate the napkin. New York!"

The *New Yorker* journalist Jane Kramer, in her memoir *The Reporter's Kitchen*, got at the downside of wieners as street food. From a vendor in Germany, she bought a grilled sausage and realized she had a mess on her hands. Mopping up required "four paper napkins and the business section of the *Frankfurter Allgemeine Zeitung*." Jim Harrison, in *The Raw and the Cooked*, wrote about cramming a hot dog into his mouth outside the Metropolitan Museum of Art. "Unfortunately, the mustard and onions cascaded down my natty outfit," he wrote. "I didn't notice this, despite all the amused stares, which I interpreted as New York bonhomie." Harrison was devoted to Gray's Papaya, the all-night NYC hot dog joint. So is the poet Paul Muldoon. Muldoon's book *Maggot* contains a poem in which the narrator notes that

> *a fallen angel serves only to perpetuate*
> *your idea that manna from heaven*
> *may be found to an unprecedented degree in Gray's*
> *Papaya at*
> *Eighth Avenue and West Thirty-seventh.*

A tour of New York City that neglects Gray's Papaya is not a tour of New York City. My favorite hot dogs are Chicago-style, "dragged through the garden," as devotees say: all-beef hot dogs with mustard, sweet relish, diced onions, tomato slices, sport peppers, a pickle spear, and celery salt on a poppy-seed bun. These used to be hard to come by in Manhattan. When I worked in Times Square, Virgil's Real Barbecue on West Forty-Fourth Street made a respectable Chicago dog, and I had one at least twice a month. A few years ago, without warning, some cretin took it off the menu.

In Larry McMurtry's very funny autobiographical novel *All My Friends Are Going to Be Strangers*, his narrator, Danny Deck, is a young novelist on the verge of fame. In one of the book's best scenes, Danny, who's from Texas, finds himself walking on Hollywood Boulevard after selling his first novel to the movies. He senses his life is about to change, in some ways for the worse. It's an oddly moving moment, one of my favorites in McMurtry's fiction:

> I walked along, staring at things, and when I got down into Hollywood I felt normal enough to be hungry and stopped and ate two chili dogs. I felt slightly rebellious. Bruce [his agent] would have been disgusted. They were great chili dogs—far superior to any I'd eaten in San Francisco. These were huge baroque L.A. chili dogs, with melted cheese and onions and even tabasco if I wanted it. I had mine with tabasco and drank a malt to cool me off. I felt like it might be my last real meal.

Ignatius, in *A Confederacy of Dunces*, operates a hot dog cart in New Orleans's French Quarter. He likes that people can select their own frank, as if they were choosing a lobster from a tank. He also likes his uniform; to him it resembles an academic robe. Ignatius eats most of his stock himself. Frederick Exley, in *A Fan's Notes*, says you should sit on the aisle at sporting events, to access the hot dog vendor. In Fairmont, I've eaten several hundred hot dogs at Yann's, a state shrine. The owner, Russell Yann, died in 2021 after spending decades over his griddle, but his daughter is keeping the place going. Yann's serves them with chili con carne, beanless and spicy, in soft steamed buns, sometimes topped with chopped onions as a flavor intensifier.

There are always a few broke, hungry West Virginians outside Yann's. When you buy a hot dog (or anything else) for someone in need, recall the advice Vivian Gornick supplies in her memoir *The Odd Woman and the City*. A man recounts to her how, as a boy, he bought a hot dog for a "bum" who was hungry. His father responded by slapping him. "If you're gonna do a thing," the father said, "do it right. You don't buy someone a hot dog without you also buying him a soda!"

* * *

Salty, fatty, crispy, and spicy: the basic food groups, essential building blocks for happiness, more all-American than apple pie. Lunch is when I eat fast food, when I do. This is Americana, democracy in a paper wrapper. It makes sense that Evel Knievel's first audiences were the diners outside at an A&W drive-in, when you ordered from a carhop instead of via a dented speaker. Maybe Jack and Diane, from the John Mellencamp song, were there, instead of sucking on chili dogs outside the Tastee Freez. "Tastee Freez in Fiction" will not be on a college syllabus anytime soon. Yet the characters in S. A. Cosby's superb Southern crime novels are obsessive about Tastee Freez double chocolate milkshakes. Chuck Klosterman, in *Fargo Rock City*, is a student of cheap thrills. "Listening to Van Halen is like having the best sex of your life with three foxy nursing students you met at a Tastee Freez," he wrote. On the other hand, listening to Eric Clapton is like "getting a sensual massage from a woman you've loved for the past ten years." Eve Babitz saw things similarly. "The Byrds and the Beach Boys and the Mamas and the Papas," she wrote, "all sounded as though they came out of a Frostie Freeze machine pipe organ."

* * *

The primal urge to consume warm, greasy food is one Orwell recognized. "When you are unemployed, which is to say when you are underfed, harassed, bored and miserable, you don't *want* to eat dull wholesome food," he wrote in *The Road to Wigan Pier*. "You want something a little bit 'tasty.' There is always some cheaply pleasant thing to tempt you. Let's have three pennorth of chips! Run out and buy us a twopenny ice-cream!" When a friend and I were on a small boat that ran out of gas in the Gulf of Mexico, and we drifted and bobbed for six hours and into the night, slowly becoming terrified we'd never be found, our food dreams ran almost entirely to McDonald's quarter-pounders with cheese and french fries.

The journalist Tommy Tomlinson, like Orwell, understands these sorts of cravings. Tomlinson didn't grow up with money. His parents made minimum wage at a seafood processing plant. "It's easy to look down on fast food," he writes in his memoir, *The Elephant in the Room*. "But it's a cheap night out of the house, and when you're poor, that counts for a lot." It's worth pausing to talk about Tomlinson for a moment. He grew up in Georgia, and he's an ardent scholar of the South's vernacular cuisine: fried chicken, biscuits, barbecue, catfish browned in flour and bacon grease, and "tea so sweet it could hold its shape without a cup." His writing makes you want to lick the page.

He was a big kid who topped out, in his thirties, at 460 pounds. His shirt size was XXXXXXL. Tomlinson would probably have been merely an M.B.G.—a Mildly Big Guy—if he didn't also have a taste for fast food. If you've ever been in a fast-food parking lot, wolfing items from a hot bag and hoping for no contemporaneous judgment of your activities, well, Tomlinson is the laureate of this experience. "On those days when the gravity of solitude tries to pin me down, fast food serves as a little bridge to the other side," he writes. He'll sit in his car and people-watch. "At least, I tell myself, I've been out among people for a while." The food "pushes the hurt down the road a little bit." He walks his readers through the succulence of the double with cheese at Wendy's: "The part I really like is out on the edge, where the meat and the cheese and the bread melt into pure umami."

Calvin Trillin used to write about his friend Fats Goldberg, a pizza shop owner who'd lost a lot of weight. "I did not get fat on coq au vin," Goldberg said. Neither did Tomlinson. Krispy Kreme doughnuts, bowls of peanut M&M's, chili dogs, Hardee's cinnamon biscuits, and sleeves of Chips Ahoy! cookies were among his fetishes. "By the time I was old enough to know anything," he writes, "I was fat." He recounts many stories of being picked on and left out. He's had, in some respects, a very good life: plenty of friends, a job he loves, a wife he adores. But he broods on the things being heavy has kept him from. "When I was a kid, I never climbed a tree or learned to swim. When I was in my twenties, I never took a girl home from a bar. Now I'm fifty, and I've never hiked a mountain or ridden a skateboard or done a cartwheel."

He has no argument with fat-positivity advocates. But he writes: "I'm just going to speak for myself. I don't want the world to expand to make room for me. It's not good for me, and it's not good for the world. I need to make myself fit." He adds: "I'm not supposed to be this big. Maybe other people are. Not me." Tomlinson goes out of his way to praise the movie critic Roger Ebert, and not just because he was "a fat guy who thrived on TV through the force of his talent." I love his book. I found myself sneak-reading it from the moment it came in the door. So many of his experiences mirror my own. As with a sack of White Castle burgers, I hated to reach the end.

\* \* \*

By now we've all read our Eric Schlosser, our Alice Waters, our Marion Nestle, our Michael Pollan. These are first-rate writers and thinkers, and God bless them, but they can't help, at times, sounding sanctimonious. We know how we should be eating. We know what's in "natural flavors," or rather what's not in them, because the FDA doesn't require food labels to tell us. Pollan has boiled his philosophy down into seven bleak words: "Eat food. Not too much. Mostly plants." We recall that Lee Harvey Oswald lived on burgers and Cokes. We darkly suspect the comedian Bill Burr was onto something when he asked, "You ever notice whenever the government fucks up, all of a sudden McDonald's has a new sandwich?" If you spend too much time in Fast Food World, you sense you're detaching from the literate world. Here, the menus are pictures, as if they were crime-scene photos. "Fast food is like cliché or computerese," Terry Eagleton has written. "Genuine eating combines pleasure, utility and sociality, and so differs from a take-away in much the same way that Proust differs from a bus ticket."

Yet because they're nearly always open, fast-food franchises are friends to writers. David Mamet's book *Writing in Restaurants* contains surprisingly little about writing in restaurants. But he wrote, "In a restaurant one is both observed and unobserved. Joy and sorrow can be displayed and observed 'unwittingly,' the writer scowling naively and the diners wondering, What the *hell* is he doing?" In pinches, on deadline, I've written in nearly every major fast-food chain. Richard Russo, who won a Pulitzer Prize for his novel *Empire Falls*, writes regularly in cafés and sometimes in a Denny's. August Wilson wrote some of the plays in his Pittsburgh Cycle at an Arthur Treacher's Fish & Chips. Nicholson Baker has worked in Friendly's, he's said.

I can't quite imagine writing in a Subway franchise, but maybe that's because I've read Campbell McGrath's poem "Woe," which begins

*Consider the human capacity for suffering,*
*our insatiable appetite for woe.*
*I do not say this lightly*
*but the sandwiches at Subway*

*suck. Foaming lettuce,*
*mayo like rancid bear grease,*
*meat the color of a dead dog's tongue.*

\* \* \*

One August morning around 2014, I wrote a book review in a Bojangles near Badin Lake in rural North Carolina. It was the only place I could find Wi-Fi. I still have a copy of the book; it smells, lingeringly, like grease and, somehow, armpits. I'm not anti–fast food, yet Bojangles makes the hairs on the back of my neck prickle. It's hard not to feel that way once you've read George Packer's book *The Unwinding: An Inner History of the New America*. In one scene, Packer finds himself talking to a farmer named Dean, who connects a lot of dots. Bojangles had come to represent for Dean everything wrong with how Americans interact with the land, with animals, and with each other. Packer writes, in one long, troubling, onrushing sentence, one you might want to read aloud:

> Some nights he sat up late on his front porch with a glass of Jack and listened to the trucks heading south on 220, carrying crates of live chickens to the slaughterhouses—always under cover of darkness, like a vast and shameful trafficking—chickens pumped full of hormones that left them too big to walk—and he thought how these same chickens might return from their destination as pieces of meat to the floodlit Bojangles' up the hill from his house, and that meat would be drowned in the bubbling fryers

by employees whose hatred of the job would leak into the cooked food, and that food would be served up and eaten by customers who would grow obese and end up in the hospital in Greensboro with diabetes or heart failure, a burden to the public, and later Dean would see them riding around the Mayodan Wal-Mart in electric carts because they were too heavy to walk the aisles of a Supercenter, just like hormone-fed chickens.

Packer's line about the hatred of the job bleeding into the food itself has stayed with me.

Fast-food uniforms, of every stripe, seem designed to be humiliating. They were especially so in the 1970s and '80s, when they were all ketchup reds and mustard yellows. Employees looked like refugees from a cult meeting, or an *Up with People* audition. I've always looked and felt ridiculous in uniforms. A friend once saw me in a Mississippi state trooper jacket that belonged to another friend's father. He didn't stop laughing for fifteen minutes, and he has made me promise to remind him of this sight to cheer him up on his deathbed.

One summer, home from college, I delivered pizzas for Domino's. I looked especially ridiculous in Domino's red, white, and blue polyester getup, with the matching gimme cap. Before I signed on, I didn't stop to think through the sartorial implications. Nor did it occur to me I'd be at the beck and call of my old high school friends and, worse, my old high school enemies. Closing up at night was awful, too: sweeping, scouring, killing bugs, removing bags of garbage. The refrain in a hit song by the Motels went, "Take the 'L' out of lover and it's over." Late at night in Domino's, mopping, listening to the radio, we amended this to "Take the 'C' out of closer and it's loser."

I do have some fond memories from Domino's. Here's one: A fellow driver was a gun fanatic with an adolescent's mustache and flag decals on his faded black Camaro. In the dead time between pizza runs, he'd stand around and blame America's problems on liberals and commies. I'm on the left; we'd razz each other while coming and going. At some point that summer, in a Miami bookstore, I stumbled on a copy of the English-language edition of *Pravda*, then the official newspaper of the Communist Party in the Soviet Union. I bought it to mess with him, and it worked. I'd ostentatiously open it every time he came around. I'd peer over the top, grinning. Do conservatives still have senses of humor? He did. He responded by bringing in back issues of *Guns & Ammo* magazine and declaiming his favorite bits out loud, as if they were Shakespearean monologues.

In Charles Wright's novel *The Wig*, the narrator winds up in a costume that steals whatever dignity he has left. He's a down-on-his-luck writer. He can't get published, and he fears he'll never be able to enter the mainstream of American life. Defeated and broke, he becomes a mascot, a "chicken man," for a chain called King of Southern Fried Chicken in Harlem. The pay is dismal and the humiliation intense. The one upside is all the fried chicken he can eat. "I was crawling through the streets of Harlem on my hands and knees, wearing a snow-white, full-feathered chicken costume," he says. "The costume was very warm. The feathers were electrified to keep people from trying to pluck them out or kicking the wearer in the tail." The electrified feathers are a typically outrageous Wright detail. The narrator continues, on his grim rounds: "I was dreaming, not of a white Christmas, I was dreaming of becoming part of The Great Society. So I went through the March streets on my hands and knees and cried:

> Cock-a-doodle-doo. Cock-a-doodle-do!
> Eat me. Eat me. All over town.
> Eat me at the King of
> Southern Fried Chicken!

In Tracie McMillan's book, *The American Way of Eating*, she goes undercover to work at an Applebee's and she reports that, before long, "I'll have learned how to spot the other members of my tribe on the subway: heavy-lidded eyes, blank stares, black pants specked with grease, hard-soled black shoes."

\* \* \*

Few writers have explored the grind of fast-food work as intimately as Atticus Lish did in *Preparation for the Next Life*, his first novel. It's an intense book with a low, flyspecked center of gravity. It's about blinkered lives, scummy apartments, dismal food, bad options. It's also an intense love story. One of this novel's two central characters is Zou Lei, who works in the kitchen of a second-rate Chinese restaurant in a Flushing, Queens, mall. She's an ethnic Uighur from northwest China, and the other workers don't understand her language. Lish boils down the routines of her job, in a way that gets at the rhythmical monotony: "Open gate, light fire, pour oil, put the kettle on, dice meat, mince meat, parse meat, make rice, make sauce, pick greens, make dough, make dumplings, make French fries, carry in goods—because I'm strong, even though I'm female. I've had military training. Take order, shout order, deliver take-out, count the till, dump trash, sweep floor, mop floor, wipe counter, wash dish, bowl, pot, dipper, cleaver, shovel, chopstick, spoon, turn out the fire, shut the light, lock the gate. Every day, work hard, sleep sweet." In one of this novel's few acts of mercy, a late-night employee lets Zou Lei and her boyfriend sleep overnight in a closed McDonald's.

In the work of the young writers Bryan Washington and Ocean Vuong, the easy availability of fast-food franchises defines their characters socioeconomically; they're short-hand for poverty and anomie. The subtle and flexible stories in Washington's *Lot* play out across Houston's sprawling and multiethnic neighborhoods. Washington places the casual racism of the food industry on display. When a young Latino man goes looking for work in a restaurant, "They read my name and they saw my face and they pointed to the dishes." Vuong's *On Earth We're Briefly Gorgeous* is set in a Hartford that has little in common with the poet Wallace Stevens's decorous, buttoned-down old New England city. Vuong pins the details of these marginalized immigrant lives, the food stamps and Goodwill stores and Thomas Kinkade images and expensive nighttime language classes and trips to the corner store for "cigarettes and Hot Cheetos."

A lot of Vuong's imagery comes from food. After a day of work in tobacco fields, the hands of his protagonist, Little Dog, who comes from a Vietnamese family, are "so thick and black with sap, dirt, pebbles, and splinters, they resembled the bottom of a pan of burned rice." In one of the best scenes in Vuong's novel, Little Dog has met an older kid who wears a John Deere cap—Little Dog calls him a "redneck"—and falls into an erotic reverie that blends food and sexuality: "I wanted more, the scent, the atmosphere of him, the taste of French fries and peanut butter underneath the salve of his tongue, the salt around his neck from the two-hour drives to nowhere and a Burger King at the edge of the county, a day of tense talk with his old man, the rust from the electric razor he shared with that old man, how I would always find it on his sink in its sad plastic case, the tobacco, weed and cocaine on his fingers mixed with motor oil, all of it accumulating into the afterscent of wood smoke caught and soaked in his hair."

What is the human soul, the great Stanley Elkin asked, but a franchise?* In Sayaka Murata's *Convenience Store Woman*, a deadpan novel from Japan, a woman senses that society finds her strange; she culls herself from the herd before anyone else can do it. She becomes an anonymous employee of the Hiiromachi Station Smile Mart, a convenience store, a kiosk for her floating soul, where she finds it easier to shout "Irasshaimase!" ("Welcome!") and "Hai!" ("Yes!") all day than to have more complicated human contact. *Convenience Store Woman* struck a chord in Japan, where it sold 1.5 million copies. Its heroine, Keiko, is thirty-six, essentially friend-

---

* Elkin mostly wrote about the disenfranchised.

less, and a virgin; she's a sort of wimple-free nun, the Smile Mart her convent. Keiko eats most of her meals there. "When I think that my body is entirely made up of food from this store," she says, "I feel like I'm as much a part of the store as the magazine racks or the coffee machine."

Biking to grade school each morning, my friends and I would pass the 7-Eleven on Third Street South in Naples. We'd fish around out back for bottles to trade in, for the nickels in deposit money, to buy candy. Slurpees came in plastic Evel Knievel and Johnny Cash cups. The Jerry Lewis telethon always seemed to be coming or going. One morning an older kid caught two lizards and put them into the 7-Eleven's busy microwave, during a lull between people nuking their frozen breakfast burritos. He pressed the "on" button and ran.

*　*　*

Most days, I eat lunch at home. I make do with what's in the house. Usually that means a sandwich—two pieces of bread, blank canvases, pale Mark Rothko slabs. I can be as geeky as the next person with the *jamón ibérico*, or with the writer Julia Reed's mother's tuna salad, but I'm also on the record as being perhaps America's most ardent consumer of the peanut butter and pickle sandwich.

It's a sandwich that my father bequeathed to me, the thrifty one that got him through law school. I wrote about the combination in 2012 for the *Times* food section. I called the sandwich the stay-at-home writer's friend, there for you when nothing else is in the icebox. My essay prompted so much grossing out on social media, then in newspapers worldwide, that I fear that when I die, should I merit even a tiny obituary, the sandwich will be mentioned near the top ("Dwight Garner, Literary Critic and Champion of Gross Sandwich, Dies at 87"). I've always assumed that the PB&P was a West Virginia thing, but I've been unable to prove it. Neither has Emily Hilliard, the former state folklorist, who tried harder than I did. The sandwich appeared on lunch-counter menus during the Depression and in extension-service cookbooks in the 1930s and '40s in recipes that generally called for a few spoonfuls of pickle relish.

Wondering why the sandwich couldn't get the respect it deserves, I emailed chefs and food writers to get their take on the combination. I expected to get high fives from this crowd, the way I would in book circles if I'd unearthed an unjustly neglected writer, another Lucia Berlin. Instead, I got crickets. A few reacted with outright disgust, the way people did when they heard Julia Roberts was marrying Lyle Lovett. Finally I found Lee Zalben, the owner of now-defunct Peanut Butter & Co. in Greenwich Village. He had a PB&P on his menu and understood, better than I did, why it works. Americans are used to peanut butter with sweet pairings—but in many older cultures it's combined with savory things, as in satays and moles.

When the food section printed my article, its editors needled me by running it with a gruesome photograph of the sandwich (squishy white bread, wan pickle slices) that seemed to have been plucked from a sun-damaged copy of *White Trash Cooking*. No disrespect to that inimitable book, but I was trying to class this combo up. David Remnick, the editor of *The New Yorker*, called me after the piece ran and said, "That sandwich is the most goyish thing I've ever seen in my life." I tried to set him straight about how to properly make one: on good toast, with first-rate pickles. He never called back.

The press wasn't all negative. A few years later, in *Slate*, Christina Cauterucci wrote that I, personally, am "a member of the rarefied club of journalists whose writing has actually moved hearts and minds on a topic of great importance. In one 2012 article, he changed my life, intimately and permanently, with an ode to an object I'd never previously considered with the solemnity it deserves: the peanut butter and pickle sandwich." Stick that in my obit.

\*  \*  \*

The other sandwich of my West Virginia youth that lives on in my mind, and in my kitchen, to Cree's dismay, is fried bologna. Robert Sietsema, the great New York City food writer, is a devotee. He once worked in a Texas hospital where there was, amazingly, "a hot vending machine that sold nothing but fried baloney sandwiches on biscuits, oozing grease and mustard." I've scoured eBay for one of these, to no avail. The fried bologna sandwich is probably the sort of dish Jonathan Gold was referring to when he wrote about "the secret ethnic cooking of the Dumb White Guy." But everyone likes them. Henry Louis Gates Jr. is an admirer. He grew up in Piedmont, West Virginia, about two hours east of where my family lived. In *Colored People*, his memoir, he wrote about a brand of bologna I wish I'd known about: Dent Davis's Famous Homemade Ring Bologna, sold at a bakery. Gates called it "one of Piedmont's singular attractions . . . dark red, with a tight, crimson, translucent skin."

Dent's bologna had a mystery ingredient. No one knew what it was, Gates wrote, adding: "Nobody white, that is." The piquant flavor apparently came from Davis's handyman, Mr. Boxie, who tended to be around when the bologna was being made. "Mr. Boxie was the dirtiest, smelliest, sloppiest, most disheveled colored man in all of Piedmont, and maybe the world," Gates wrote. "The town said Mr. Boxie was *funky*, long before Motown or James Brown thought of making 'funky' mean cool, hip, or 'down.' No, Mr. Boxie was funky because he smelled bad." After Gates learned the truth about his favorite sandwich, he went to his father. "Tell me it ain't so, Pop." His reply came: "It's so, boy." Gates's story reminds me of Harryette Mullen's poem "Muse and Drudge," the one in which she writes,

> *when you get food this good*
> *you know the cook stuck her foot in it*

The fried bologna sandwich has made a comeback. I've had quite posh versions, made with artisanal mortadella, the thinking man's bologna, in Manhattan restaurants. They're on the menu at Turkey and the Wolf in New Orleans, a sandwich shop that, in 2017, *Bon Appétit* called the best new restaurant in America. I'd still rather eat one out of a vending machine in Texas.

\* \* \*

"The correct drink for fried bologna *à la Nutley, Nouveau Jersey*," the *Times* columnist Russell Baker wrote, "is a 1927 Nehi Cola." I have a childhood predisposition for Nehi, usually grape, which I'd drink so rapidly it would backfire up my nose. I allow myself a few bottles a year now. I'll put one in the back of the fridge and stare at it longingly for a month, until the moment seems ripe. I'll crack it open at lunchtime, with a sandwich. It's never quite as good as I'd remembered. Soda tastes best when you're young, a fact attested to by Eve Babitz in *Slow Days, Fast Company*. "Chocolate Cokes in high school are better than caviar on a yacht when you're forty-five," she wrote. "It's common knowledge."

I'm in thrall to Diet Coke and drink several cans a day. I mostly buy the 7.5-ounce minis though they're more expensive. It took me years to realize that what I'm usually after isn't a can of Diet Coke but the *first three glugs* of a can of Diet Coke. Donald Trump is a Diet Coke fiend, and the connection rattles me. He is said to drink two six-packs a day. I would have sold my stock in Coca-Cola when I learned that, if I'd owned stock in Coca-Cola. Lyndon Johnson is the president to respect, in soda consumption terms. He liked Fresca so much he had a summoning button installed on his desk in the Oval Office. We can be grateful LBJ kept the Fresca button distinct from the nuclear attack button.

In her novel *God Help the Child*, Toni Morrison delivered this put-down: "My sex life became sort of like Diet Coke—deceptively sweet minus nutrition." Tennessee Williams is the laureate of Coca-Cola. It's everywhere in his plays, especially in *A Streetcar Named Desire*. "Run to the drugstore and get me a lemon-coke with plenty of chipped ice in it!" Blanche says to Stella. When Stella brings her the drink, Blanche asks, "Is that coke for me? . . . Why, you precious thing, you! Is it just coke?" Stella asks, "You mean you want a shot in it!" Blanche replies, "Well, honey, a shot never does a coke any harm!"

There are ways to smuggle Nehi onto your dinner table. Vertamae Smart-Grosvenor, in her classic book, *Vibration Cooking*, prints a recipe for smothered chicken given to her by the Mississippi-born painter Joe Overstreet. Here it is in its entirety: "Salt and pepper the cut-up chicken. Shake in a paper bag in flour. Fry in oil until golden brown. Remove excess grease and add 1 bottle orange soda pop. Cover and smother for 15 minutes." The sweetness almost entirely bubbles away. Willie Mays, who was a teetotaler, had a standard order in a bar: a soft drink with six cherries, a slice of lemon, and a straw. According to James S. Hirsch, his biographer, bartenders would "tease him that the cherries would get him drunk."

\* \* \*

I was happy to recently learn that, when you order a croque monsieur, the classic French ham and cheese sandwich made with Gruyère, ham, and a simple béchamel sauce, you are essentially asking for a Mister Crunchy. A lunky boyfriend in Gael Greene's sex-and-food novel *Blue Skies, No Candy*, asks, "What is a croak monsieur?" French sandwiches are better than American sandwiches, as a rule, because the bread is better. In his novel *The Committed*, the Vietnamese American writer Viet Thanh Nguyen considers what he calls "that dialectical baguette." He's probing Vietnam's complicated relationship with France, its former colonizer. He owns up to the warring voices in his mind. "Oh, baguette!" he writes. "Symbol of France, and hence symbol of French colonialization! So spoke one side of me. But the other side said, at the same time, Ah, baguette! Symbol of how we Vietnamese have made French culture our own! For we were good bakers of the baguette, and the banh mi we created with baguettes were far tastier and more imaginative than the sandwiches the French fashioned from them." Banh mi are crucial to have in your repertoire, especially at lunch—keep the basic fixings around—because they are among the simplest yet stunning things you can make with leftover meat.

The stealth ingredient in a good banh mi, of course, is mayonnaise. Lunch is when the bulk of one's mayo consumption occurs. Surely Barbara Kingsolver was right to comment, in her novel *Unsheltered*: "Hell is other people, with egg salad." Sylvia Plath, her diaries make plain, was a devoted consumer of tuna salad sandwiches. In an earthy entry from 1956, she wrote: "Exhausted; lifted skirt under bridge, behind truck, secure in noise of falling water and urinated on sidewalk; ate greasy good last of tuna sandwich." It is tuna's bad luck that we find them so tasty. As Lorrie Moore wrote, in her collection of stories *Bark*, "If dolphins tasted good, . . . we wouldn't even know about their language." Mayonnaise comes at you in potato salad, as well. "Potato salad in the South is nothing less than the principal smuggler of cholesterol into the festive, careless heart," Padgett Powell wrote in *Edisto*, his first novel. "It is pure poison beneath the facade of bland puritan propriety. It is the food of choice at any fond banquet of smiling relatives who celebrate tacitly among themselves the dark twining of two of their promising youth." Powell wrote a 164-page novel, *The Interrogative Mood*, in which every sentence is a question. (Sample: "Have you decided yet which historical moment you would most like to have witnessed with your own eyes and ears?") The form suited Powell, because he's one of the most inquisitive writers we have.

When I'm hungover, menudo is my lunchtime accomplice. Good menudo is a chore to make; it requires the collection of cow's feet, marrow bones, and tripe. But in Harlem there are two good versions within a few blocks. Ray Gonzalez, in his memoir *Memory Fever: A Journey Beyond* El Paso del Norte, catches the enthusiasm a good bowl produces. "An innocent, ignorant person would say it looks like dog vomit and leftover cooking grease! But you love it and that person will never know the meaning of life," he writes, adding: "You slurp it like an anteater slurps ants, like a vacuum cleaner slurps dirt, like a monkey eats bananas, like a man slurps himself into sleep to wake up in search of his mama."

When I can't muster the energy to cook at lunch, I make a baptismal bowl of Campbell's tomato soup, from the can. I grew up on it. Cree won't touch the stuff; she finds it too sweet. I use whole milk and add a pat of butter. Ideally this is consumed alongside a grilled cheese sandwich. It's redolent of all that is good in the world. In *The Making of the President 1960*, Theodore H. White reported that, while boarding a plane after campaigning in West Virginia, John F. Kennedy "called for a favorite drink—a bowl of hot tomato soup."

\* \* \*

There are big lunches, and there are landslide lunches. In 2014 I was invited to consume, and write about, the lunch of a lifetime: a fifty-course meal in Seattle, prepared by Nathan Myhrvold, the Microsoft multimillionaire turned cookbook writer, for his culinary hero, Ferran Adrià, the Catalan chef who pioneered molecular gastronomy at El Bulli, his avant-garde restaurant on the Costa Brava. Molecular gastronomy seems dated now, and very 2008. But when I learned I'd be sitting in at this meal for seven, to write about it for *T: The New York Times Style Magazine*, I felt I'd won the lottery, and not the Shirley Jackson kind. Trepidation set in, too. Could I handle fifty courses? Some of my close friends are bons vivants on an almost professional scale—people for whom eating less, or drinking less, or going to bed before anyone else would be a profound admission of defeat. I gave up competing long ago. While A. J. Liebling is among my heroes, I understand what his *New Yorker* colleague Brendan Gill was complaining about when he wrote that Liebling thought that "eating two or three times as much as I was" clearly made him "a better man than I." Liebling, who was obese, died young, at fifty-nine. He chose a short, glorious life, at the table, over a long undistinguished one.

Adrià and Myhrvold made for an odd couple. Adrià is compact and handsome in an Antonio Banderas–meets–Leonard Cohen manner. When he tastes something he likes, he closes his eyes and says, "Fantástico." Myhrvold resembles a cartoon chipmunk, the kind that laughs when you poke its tummy.* The two were at the top of the so-called modernist

---

* He was in a jollier mood then, before his name bubbled up in connection to Jeffrey Epstein, the late financier and sex offender.

cuisine, one that pushed chefs and intrepid home cooks to master a new batterie de cuisine (sous vide vacuum sealers, ultrasonic homogenizers, centrifuges) and to fill their pantries with avant-garde chemical staples like xanthan gum and liquid lecithin.

Between 2005 and 2011, Myhrvold had flown halfway around the world many times to eat at El Bulli. He took Adrià's ideas back home and began to experiment with them. Cooking out of a lab on the outskirts of Seattle that also houses his patent-generating company, he and a battalion of chefs produced a six-volume, 2,438-page slab of a book titled *Modernist Cuisine: The Art and Science of Cooking*. The book has been influential—it provided the first truly thorough explication of sous vide cooking—and went through several printings despite its $625 price tag. Myhrvold began hosting dinners in his lab for friends like Bill Gates, Thomas Keller, and David Chang. Other chefs flew into town for these meals, which would comprise as many as thirty labor-intensive courses. It was America's most elite pop-up. The person Myhrvold most wanted to cook for was Adrià. When he learned his idol would be in Seattle, he proposed fifty courses in homage to a similar meal he'd had at El Bulli. Adrià accepted.

\* \* \*

We sat down at Myhrvold's table, under fluorescent lights, at 1:00 p.m. on a gray Friday afternoon. At each place setting was a copy of Myhrvold's menu, with dishes that ran down the pages like the technical credits at the end of a James

Cameron movie. The first two courses, served by a staff hired for the event, were deconstructed cocktails. Myhrvold's "Bloody Mary" resembled a stick of celery with a dollop of mayo piped on top. Popped into the mouth though, it expanded. The mayo was alcoholic—Everclear and milk emulsified into oil. On top were microcubes of clam-juice gel, as well as tiny juice sacs from a lime that had been cryo-frozen and then shattered. The cocktail was dusted with tomato powder, horseradish, salt, and pepper. It was one of the best things I've ever put into my mouth.

Myhrvold likes the rigor of complicated food, to which he applies the same principles as his other projects. In a room not far from where we ate, a laser was aimed at a wire box swarming with mosquitoes. To fight malaria, the lab had invented a device that identifies, tracks, and zaps female mosquitoes (only females bite humans). An inventor with hundreds of patents who also has a way with oysters is a rarity in our world. The oysters in question, Kumamotos, had been "cryo-shucked"—that is, plunged into liquid nitrogen for fifteen seconds to pop their shells like automobile hoods. Muscles that attached the bivalves to the shells had been ripped away, as if via bikini wax. The shells themselves had been sandblasted, to polish them, in the lab's shop. The oysters were served, two nestled in each half shell, along with pearls of a puree made from sunchokes, oysters, and brine. For acidity, a sprinkle of lemon gelée was added. They were delicious—but not more so than the best briny East Coast oysters. We were off and running. The dishes began to come, each as small and complex as a flower, some served as single bites on white Chinese soupspoons. A dish called "Milagro al Pastor" arrived with tortillas laser-cut with an image of Adrià's face. During the "Asia" courses, two types of fish, escolar and ahi, were combined to make a chessboard. In "France," what appeared to be caviar was a cluster of pressure-cooked mustard seeds with squid ink and other ingredients. "Fantástico," Adrià said.

A common critique of Myhrvold's food is that it's pedantic. Yet when Myhrvold uses a centrifuge, for example, to whir out the essence of peas or carrots for his dishes, the results are, well, fantástico. I learned early in the meal that Myhrvold likes to salt his wine. He does so because he thinks salt can balance a wine's flavors, especially those that are tannic, but also because it's a way to freak out the hidebound. By the time we'd had thirty-eight courses, I was full. After forty-five courses, I was lowing, and worried about what condition my condition was in. I felt like the painter J. M. W. Turner, who famously lashed himself to a ship's mast to experience a snowstorm. I began to meditate on the notion of death by remorseless beauty. The final dish, an absinthe cocktail topped with a swirling sugar mold made with a 3D printer, arrived after 6:00 p.m. Adrià downed his absinthe and began to wonder where he might go for dinner that night.

I wasn't hungry again until midnight. That's when I ducked out of my hotel room for a cheeseburger at Dick's, the indispensable Seattle burger joint. No amount of twiddling could improve upon it. Myhrvold's meal had left me feeling curiously empty. I didn't speak Spanish and Adrià didn't speak English. Our conversation, through a translator, was strained. The fluorescent lights didn't help. Nor did the fact that the other five people around the table were publicists with little to add to the conversation. There was no conviviality, no banter, no jokes, no music. It felt like an autopsy. Mentally I've filed it as, unless I get to select the company, a supposedly fun thing I'll never do again.

* * *

Myhrvold got one thing right. At the start of a big meal, oysters are what you want. I came to them late. Like coffee and alcohol and the music of John Coltrane, raw oysters can be off-putting at first. Like coffee and alcohol and the music of John Coltrane, they can come to be among the things you live for. It wouldn't be hard to create an anthology of essays in which writers sample their first oyster. It's a rite of initiation.

Anton Chekhov, as a boy, was terrified of them. He was sure they'd resemble nasty frogs, "peeping out from it with big, glittering eyes . . . and a slimy skin." In *The Gastronomical Me*, M. F. K. Fisher describes being in high school when a teacher carried in a platter of bluepoints. She shuddered. "I knew that I would be sick if I had to swallow anything in the world alive, but especially a live oyster." The narrator of Stephanie Danler's novel *Sweetbitter* feared her first one, too. "The first oyster was a cold lozenge to push past, to push down, to take behind the taste buds in the back hollow of the throat," she said. The narrator immediately wants more, as if it's her first tattoo.

East Coast oysters, like Wellfleets, bite the wallet. You can't afford to eat them by the pail, the way you can in New Orleans, where the larger and less delicate Gulf Coast oysters are about a buck a throw. Louisiana oysters are, in A. J. Liebling's memorable phrase, "solace to a man of moderate means." Louisiana's oyster culture is intense. Michael Ondaatje's best novel, *Coming Through Slaughter*, is about the pathbreaking cornetist Buddy Bolden. It includes a scene in a nightclub during which a woman known as Olivia the Oyster Dancer "would place a raw oyster on her forehead and lean back and shimmy it down all over her body without ever dropping it . . . Then she would kick it high into the air and would catch it on her forehead and begin again." I was unable to find a contemporary oyster dancer during my time in New Orleans.

To not like oysters, in fiction, invariably marks you as a rube; it's seen as almost a moral fault. But not everyone likes them. Nabokov didn't. In *The Great Santini*, Bull Meecham, speaking for millions, refers to them as "shelled snot." Roy Blount Jr. has written that he only likes them "fried. / Then I'm sure my oyster died." Getting a bad oyster, though rare, is a nightmare. Samuel Pepys wrote in his diary, "I was sick and was forced to vomit up my oysters again and then I was well." More than a few writers have demonstrated a certain sympathy with the oyster. "Do you appreciate that an oyster has, among its other organs, a *heart*?" Padgett Powell asked in *The Interrogative Mood*. P. G. Wodehouse wrote that "life for these unfortunate bivalves must be one damn thing after another." At a key moment in his novel *Bad News*, Edward St. Aubyn writes: "The shock of standing again under the wide pale sky, completely exposed. This must be what the oyster feels when the lemon juice falls."

*　*　*

My love of oysters has taken a toll on me. When I was in my thirties and newly employed at the *Times*, I had an after-work ritual. One night a week, before boarding a train at Grand Central, I'd stop at Jimmy's Corner, a boxing bar, for a martini. The bartender, Mike, had studied with the novelist John Gardner and had good stories on tap. Then I'd hit the Grand Central Oyster Bar for a glass of wine and a dozen Cotuits or Malpeques. When I got home, my wife was working on recipes for her first cookbook, which was about steak. Gin, wine, oysters, meat: that's a toxic brew for someone genetically predisposed as I am—though, poignantly, I did not know it at the time—to gout.

Gout sounds like it's from the Middle Ages, or Tolkien's Middle-earth. I wish it were. Instead, it's a variety of inflammatory arthritis. When your blood has elevated uric acid levels, from diet and/or genetics, that acid will crystallize. These crystals head for your joints, usually the big toe. Once lodged there, they settle in for a long and demented siege. The classic description of a gout attack comes from the English physician Thomas Sydenham, writing in 1683: "The victim goes to bed and sleeps in good health. About two o'clock in the morning he is awakened by a severe pain in the great toe . . . The pain, which was at first moderate, becomes more intense . . . Now it is a violent stretching and tearing of the ligaments—now it is a gnawing pain, and now a pressure and tightening. So exquisite and lively meanwhile is the feeling of the part affected that it cannot bear the weight of bedclothes nor the jar of a person walking in the room."

I remember my first attack as if it were twenty minutes instead of twenty years ago. It was the middle of the night. I'd gone to sleep after a version of the dining ritual described above. I awoke to a screaming coming across my foot. The big toe on my right foot was cherry red and swollen, a clown's nose. It felt as if someone had taken a flat nail and driven it, like Vulcan, through the toe's midpoint. If a puff of wind blew over this toe, or a sheet grazed it, I whimpered like a baby. Many men—gout mostly afflicts men, though women are not immune from its ravages—have tried to describe the pain. Robert Stone was a sufferer; so were Joseph Conrad, Mark Twain, Henry James, Ernest Hemingway, A. J. Liebling, Karl Marx, Richard Burton, and John Updike's character Henry Bech. Benjamin Franklin wrote a dialogue with his gout, during which all he could sometimes utter was "Eh! Oh! Eh!"

Nathaniel Hawthorne likened the feeling of having gout to being thumbscrewed, on the toe. William Golding (*Lord of the Flies*), referring to the cheerfully macabre *New Yorker* cartoonist, said it felt like something "out of Charles Addams." Jim Harrison likened the feeling to being shot in the toe by someone using a silencer. It's the kind of agony, he wrote, "where you limp toward the bathroom calling out for pets that died in your youth." It takes a certain amount of courage to out oneself as a member of what the novelist Geoff Nicholson has called the "gout community." Gout, by its reputation, if not its reality, is something that afflicts wealthy fat people.

Dick Cheney: gout man. People rarely feel sorry for you when you have it. Instead, they stifle chuckles. Surely, they think, you've brought this on yourself.

Reader, I did bring it on myself. In part I have my father to thank for this joker in the pack of my genetic burden; he's a sufferer, too. But I'm a big eater and have never been possessed of either an El Greco thinness or a strong impulse toward exercise. The list of foods doctors advise a gout sufferer to avoid sound like my idea of a good night out: anchovies, trout, bacon, veal, asparagus, kidneys, goose, scallops, brains, crab, duck, eel, tongue, tripe, and alcohol of most varieties. When my gout attacks arrived, I mentally pleaded guilty to what Eve Babitz has called, in a different context, "squalid overboogie."

My gout is gone now. I've been attack-free for many years. For this I thank a wonder pill, allopurinol, which I take daily. "There are times when only a sick man knows how warm and bright the rest of the world is," Aravind Adiga writes in his novel *Selection Day*. For this lesson, gout, my nemesis, I thank you.

# 3
# SHOPPING

On some level, I'm always full of Girl Scout
cookies.

—**TERRANCE HAYES,** *American Sonnets*
*for My Past and Future Assassin*

Let's go to the grocery store and grab a few things. I'm in sweatpants and a moth-eaten cardigan and flip-flops, so I'll hope not to run into an old frenemy. I prefer to go in late morning when market aisles are minimally populated and gleaming, the shelves are freshly stocked. Even my local Stop & Shop, at 11:00 a.m., is a snort of middlebrow surrealism. When you shop in the morning, there's time to return home and plant a few encouraging seeds (marinating, brining, defrosting) to harvest later. These secondary activities simmer in the background of the day, adding promise. If you've received bad news from a friend, or a bill that will be difficult to pay, recall A. J. Liebling's wisdom: "A good meal in troubled times is always that much salvaged from disaster." Today a morning shop isn't possible (deadline), so afternoon it shall be.

So long and cold are the aisles of modern markets, the narrator of Sigrid Nunez's novel *What Are You Going Through* thinks, that it would be a thrill to push down them on ice skates. In my dreams I've glided this way, frictionless and free, as if in a dream of flying. "The whole store was like a pinball machine," John Updike wrote in his story "A&P." You never know the aisle from which someone—your student-loan officer, your momentarily lost toddler, a zombie—will emerge.

One writer I take with me, mentally, into markets, is Émile Zola. His *The Belly of Paris*, published in 1873, is Western literature's great groceries novel. There's nothing else like it. Zola's novel is set largely in Les Halles, the sprawling and now defunct Paris food market. It's about Florent, an unjustly imprisoned convict, who escapes and finds work there as a fish inspector. The novel skates on a political knife's edge. The thin, poetical Florent is disgusted with bourgeois society—"Respectable people . . . What bastards!" he thinks—and with the self-satisfaction of a populace grown plump. Yet the book's beating heart resides in Zola's lush, funny, and erotically charged descriptions of Les Halles' bounty: cheeses, charcuterie, offal, game birds, and mountains of things like black radishes and coral-pink carrots. This is a book in which dinner conversation bends toward topics like the winter salting of meats, and in which even dawn has a "balsamic scent."

What would it have been like to shop alongside Zola? He was the panjandrum of the produce section. The *Times* critic Anatole Broyard published a collection of reviews titled *Aroused by Books*. Zola was aroused by fruit. In *The Belly of Paris* he described apples with the "ruddy glow of budding breasts." The skins of peaches resembled "necks of brunettes at the nape." Zola was high-strung company in the cheese aisle, as well. A disk of Gruyère resembled "a wheel fallen from some barbarian chariot." Circles of Brie were "melancholy extinct moons." Zola is hardly alone in tapping into the eroticism of markets. Allen Ginsberg, in "A Supermarket in California," wrote voyeuristically about Walt Whitman, who was his own kind of voyeur.

> *I saw you, Walt Whitman, childless, lonely old*
> *grubber, poking among the meats in the refrigera-*
> *tor and eyeing the grocery boys.*
> *I heard you asking questions of each: Who killed*
> *the pork chops? What price bananas? Are you my*
> *Angel?*

Fran Ross, in her stinging comic novel *Oreo*, suggests in nearly sexual terms the loss of control her narrator feels in a well-stocked market. In his memoir *Lucky Bruce*, Bruce Jay Friedman described the pangs he feels shopping alongside glowing young mothers, those "home-wreckers who assemble at my local Whole Foods at five in the afternoon."

I have a shopping list; a pen is gripped between my teeth. The pen will inevitably fail to work or fall and roll in a panko-coating of grit. Inevitably, too, the crucial item on my list will be sold out, so I must make enormous changes at the last minute. A few shopping lists are famous. One from Michelangelo survives. In the spring of 1518 he needed bread, fresh anchovies, and wine. A 1609 shopping list from Galileo survives, too, written on the back of a letter. Galileo desired, among other things, rice, spices, and sugar. Maybe he wanted a rice pudding. I hang on to shopping lists from memorable meals. I tuck them into the back pages of cookbooks or novels, where I find them years later, wondering what Cree or I was thinking, putting pork belly on everything.

*   *   *

You glide into the produce section as if you were on a cushion of air, like a table-hockey puck. These are friendly industrial nursing homes; everything is on life support. My progress is usually stymied by a fortified emplacement of watermelons, uglified by orange stickers. I'm ridiculed by my family for my inability to pick watermelons. The ones I lug home, once opened, are feeble and wan, deserved outcasts. Staring into the bin, I try to summon the advice I've absorbed. "Take that which yields the lowest tone when struck with your knuckles, i.e., which is hollowest," Thoreau wrote. "The old or ripe ones sing bass; the young, tenor or falsetto." Falsetto? Beware the Bon Iver melon!

Can you hire a watermelon advisor? Elif Batuman, in her memoir *The Possessed: Adventures with Russian Books and the People Who Read Them*, meets a young man who tells her, "A good watermelon had to have an orange spot, to show where it had sat in the sun, and a dry belly button, to show that the vine had broken naturally. When you tapped it with your right hand, it had to resonate against your left hand. As to the rind, the important thing wasn't the color itself, but the contrast between the different colors." So, I tap. I scrutinize color contrast. I listen to the Russians about such things. As Janet Malcolm put it in *Iphigenia in Forest Hills*, "It is in the blood of Russian storytelling to take note of the fruit."

The best melons come from freelance vendors. "Street fruit," my daughter will say, when I ask where she got the luscious one. She knows to look for what Cree calls "the field spot." Jessica Harris, in her book *High on the Hog*, remembers a peddler on her street in Bedford-Stuyvesant, Brooklyn, when she was growing up. She dug his sign, which read: WATERMELON SWEET LIKE YOUR WOMAN. In *Zami*, Audre Lorde recalled growing up in Harlem and seeing watermelons hawked from— her writing in *Zami* is always this good—"a rickety wooden pickup truck with the southern road-dust still on her slatted sides, from which a young bony Black man with a turned-around baseball cap on his head would hang and half-yell, half-yodel—"Wahr—deeeeeee-mayyyyyyy-lawnnnnnnn."

Don't take your fondness for watermelon too far. In Cormac McCarthy's *Suttree*, an anguished farmer complains, "You ain't goin to believe this . . . Somebody has been fuckin my watermelons . . . Damn near screwed the whole patch." The farmer takes the man to court; the charge is bestiality. But the man gets off, so to speak, and brags, "My lawyer told em a watermelon wasnt no beast." I've always assumed McCarthy's scene was whimsy, that no one shagged fruit. Then I read Eugene Walter's memoir, *Milking the Moon*. Walter was a Southerner, a big eater, and a founder of *The Paris Review*. "I have never humped a melon," he wrote. "But everybody I know has humped a melon."

*       *       *

Access to good fruit, in fiction, has long been a status marker. In *The Great Gatsby*, a book so smoothly written you could spread its paragraphs on toast, Nick Carraway says about Jay Gatsby, his prosperous new neighbor: "Every Friday five crates of oranges and lemons arrived from a fruiterer in New York—every Monday these same oranges and lemons left his back door in a pyramid of pulpless halves." In *To the Lighthouse*, published two years later, in 1927, Virginia Woolf described an "arrangement of the grapes and pears, of the horny pink-lined shell, of the bananas" so beautiful that it reminds an onlooker of "a trophy fetched from the bottom of the sea."

Neil Klugman, the bright but schlubby narrator of Philip Roth's *Goodbye, Columbus*, realizes that he's a far socioeconomic cry from home when he confronts the superabundance of fresh fruit in Brenda Patimkin's house. Neil had met Brenda, back for the summer from Radcliffe, at his cousin's suburban country club. "Fruit grew in their refrigerator and sporting goods dropped from their trees," Neil says. The couple go dancing and they return to Brenda's parents' house. "We filled a bowl with cherries which we carried into the TV room," Neil tells us, "and ate sloppily for a while; and later, on the sofa, we loved each other and when I moved from the darkened room to the bathroom I could always feel cherry pits against my bare soles."

I pause by the apple display. I scan for a Cox's Orange Pippin, known in England as Cox, because the narrator of Iris Murdoch's novel *The Sea, the Sea* is obsessed with them. He's an unpretentious eater, as was Murdoch, but he has an aristocratic taste for apples: "I can eat only Cox's Orange Pippins," he says, "and am in mourning applewise from April to

October." I've never seen a Cox in an American supermarket, but I'm on perpetual alert. I'm made to feel like a dainty little man when I eat an apple because, unlike my wife, I don't crunch down the entire thing, seeds, stem, and all. Karl Ove Knausgaard's narrator in *My Struggle* does the same thing. Cree swallows the seeds in papayas and the pits in plums and cherries, too. To spit them out would impede her rat-a-tat-tat enjoyment. She's like Chekhov, who wrote about cherries in an 1897 letter, "I pick twenty at a time and stuff them all into my mouth at once. They taste better like that." She's a monster.

In the citrus section, I take two red-fleshed Cara Caras and drop them in the cart. They're a treat in Paula Wolfert's Moroccan orange salad, which has black olives. Oranges and black olives, who knew? I'm reminded of a line in Annia Ciezadlo's excellent book *Day of Honey*, about civilian life in Beirut and Baghdad during wartime, in which she asked: "What God leant down and whispered in what mortal ear to put walnuts inside an eggplant?" Cara Caras are large. Jessica Mitford's mother told her that giving birth "feels like an orange being forced up your nostril."

In *A Tramp Abroad*, Mark Twain writes about a schooner that wrecked off the coast of Scotland in the 1870s. In its holds were a vast number of oranges. The locals helped the captain rescue most of his cargo, and to thank them he said: Take all the oranges you want. The next day, the captain asked how they liked them. There was silence. At last, someone spoke up and said, "Baked, they were tough; and even boiled, they warn't things for a hungry man to hanker after." The West Virginian in me is in sync with this story. During the Depression, relief trains filled with grapefruit came into Appalachia, and people had no idea what to do with them. People ate them raw and thought their mouths would never unpucker. Archie's family tried to boil them, he told me. They fried slices in grease. West Virginians have long cultural memories. Grapefruit is as popular there as solar power.

Grapefruit loathers relish the scene in *The Public Enemy* when Jimmy Cagney mashes one into Mae Clarke's nagging face. Out of cultural loyalty, I don't eat a lot of grapefruit. Cree's a connoisseur who can distinguish between varieties, which tend to have names—"Ruby Red," "Flame," "Ray Ruby," "Pummelo HB," "Rio Star"—like Tejano musicians. I like mangoes, but I am allergic to their skin, which makes my own skin swell up, especially on my face. Just thinking about it makes me run my fingers madly up and down my arms. I'd rather be tossed into a pit of earwigs than into a pit of mangoes.

\* \* \*

I take some blackberries packaged in a clear vented plastic clamshell, remembering (for once) to check for mold. Shopping well is a skill I don't entirely possess. The best shopper I'm aware of, or the one that's the most improving to read about, at any rate, is Nella Last, whose wartime diaries— the edition I own is titled *Nella Last's War: A Mother's Diary, 1939–45*—are terrific; they're unsentimental and have an earthy power. We watch Last work, and scheme, to keep her family fed in England during a time of rationing and privation. In her memoir *The Gastronomical Me*, M. F. K. Fisher describes a similarly gifted shopper, a Madame Biarnet, at work in Dijon. "Storekeepers automatically lowered their prices when they saw her coming," Fisher wrote, "but even so she would poke sneeringly at the best bananas, say, and then demand to be shown what was in reserve."

Cree's this kind of shopper. All of Manhattan is her backyard. She sniffs and samples, peeks and palpates. She's demanding and charming, and butchers and fishmongers take to her immediately. I lack the haggling personality. When I sniff and peek and palpate, no one's eyes twinkle; I'm merely some shopkeeper's problem. I don't shop as carefully as Cree, and grocers sense this about me. I fear I resemble Dora Spenlow, David's wife in *David Copperfield*. "Our appearance in a shop was a signal for the damaged goods to be brought out immediately," David says. "If we bought a lobster, it was full of water. All our meat turned out to be tough, and there was hardly any crust to our loaves." I go home and, in my mind, write the grocer a strongly worded letter of complaint.

Blackberries are the poet's berry. Summer's blood is in them, Seamus Heaney told us in "Blackberry-Picking." Yusef Komunyakaa described how "They left my hands like a printer's / Or thief's before a police blotter." For Sylvia Plath, in "Blackberrying," they are foreboding:

> *Big as the ball of my thumb, and dumb as eyes*
> *Ebon in the hedges, fat*
> *With blue-red juices. These they squander on*
>     *my fingers.*

*I had not asked for such a blood sisterhood; they must love me.*

Here are the bananas, hung from hooks. The opening sentence of Thomas Pynchon's novel *Gravity's Rainbow* is well-known: "A screaming comes across the sky." It's a reference to Germany's fearsome V-2 rockets, the first long-range guided ballistic missiles, the so-called vengeance weapon. These rockets are compared to steel bananas, and on the Allied side Captain Geoffrey ("Pirate") Prentice is famous for growing bananas in a hothouse; they're so large that bunches resemble chandeliers. He is also famous for his banana breakfasts. He grills bananas; he fries them; he purees them in milk; he's obsessed. A breakfast scene builds. Then a cook named Osbie Feel grabs a banana and sticks it out of the fly of his striped pajama bottoms. He strokes it in 4/4 time, while singing

> *Time to gather your arse up off the floor,*
> > *(have a bana-na)*
> *Brush your teeth and go toddling off to war.*
> *Wave your hand to sleepy land,*
> *Kiss those dreams away,*
> *Tell Miss Grable you're not able,*
> *Not till V-E Day, oh,*
> *Ev'rything'll be grand in Civvie Street*
> > *(have a bana-na)*
> *Bubbly wine and girls wiv lips so sweet—*
> *But there's still the German or two to fight,*
> *So show us a smile that's shiny bright,*
> *And then, as we may have suggested once before—*
> *Gather yer blooming arse up off the floor!*

A rocket does indeed land, but not close enough to harm anyone. The alert goes out: "Banana Breakfast is saved." This is a message that a meal always imparts: Life, for now, will go on.

* * *

I push past the onions and put two leeks into my cart. I like to slice off the tops, when cooking with them, and set them on the windowsill, where the crazy tendrils wave like Struwwelpeter's hair in the children's book by Heinrich Hoffmann. Impermanent artworks, they'll last a week or two. I take some arugula. In Jonathan Franzen's novel *The Corrections*, a failed academic named Chip eats arugula that's "so strong it made his eyes water, like a paragraph of Thoreau." Arugula wasn't well-known in America before the eighties. When farmers began to grow it in California, they didn't know how much to charge. Cree's father, Bruce, explained that in Europe the cost was roughly equal to a pack of cigarettes. According to Joyce Goldstein, in her book *Inside the California Food Revolution*, farmers listened to him and initially pegged arugula prices to the cost of Bruce's Lucky Strikes.

The refreshing salad I eat almost daily has no arugula (or lettuce) in it at all: thinly sliced English cucumber with cherry tomatoes and feta cheese, with a splash of fresh olive oil and salt and pepper. Samuel Johnson would not have been impressed. "A cucumber should be well sliced, and dressed with pepper and vinegar," he said, "and then thrown out, as good for nothing." Ann Beattie has said that her last meal would include endive, though not in a calorie-saving way.

"You cut the endive in half," she explained, "hollow out a few leaves, and fill them with triple cream cheese."

I scan for watercress; it's never here. I have, in my phone somewhere, the recipe for Alice Waters's famous watercress soup, which I've never made because I can never find watercress when it's on my mind. It's a simple soup, and inexpensive to make. Yet Richard Brautigan, in *Revenge of the Lawn*, zeroed in on the class politics of watercress. "Whenever I see watercress, which isn't very often, I think of the rich," he wrote. "I think they are the only people who can afford it and they use watercress in exotic recipes that they keep hidden in vaults from the poor."

Cabbage is, somehow, watercress's plebeian opposite. John Updike, writing about Vladimir Nabokov, understood this. Updike said it seems wrong to call Nabokov an "American writer" because that phrase "fetches to mind Norman Mailer and James Jones and other homegrown cabbages loyally mistaken for roses." I always seem to be eating cabbage, because I'm always embarking on the awful cabbage soup diet. On diets I lose weight slowly, because I obey the Kingsley Amis Rule, which dictates: "The first, indeed the only, requirement of a diet is that it should lose you weight without reducing your alcoholic intake by the smallest degree."

I like the smell of sauerkraut, which of course is made from cabbage, because it generally indicates that sausages are nearby. "What is a recipe for sauerkraut doing in my notebook?" Joan Didion asked, in her classic essay, "On Keeping a Notebook." She remembers why the recipe is there, and her essay ends this way: "I was on Fire Island when I first made that sauerkraut, and it was raining, and we drank a lot of bourbon and ate the sauerkraut and went to bed at ten, and I listened to the rain and the Atlantic and felt safe. I made the sauerkraut again last night and it did not make me feel any safer, but that is, as they say, another story."

It's a very Didion moment, detecting peril in the everyday, with a side of glamour (Fire Island) and sex (too much bourbon). This passage is doubly interesting when you recall that she calls her notebook not a factual record but a compilation of "what some would call lies." I'm not suggesting Didion is "lying" in the passage above. But sauerkraut takes days if not weeks to properly ferment, and she seems to make hers on a single rainy afternoon. Either way, I believe that had Didion stared at chopped cabbage hard enough, it would have mortified into sauerkraut on the spot.

I love potatoes. I try to abstain from them, though Wittgenstein wrote that he thought best while peeling them. Jessica Mitford, whose *The American Way of Death* is among my favorite works of reportage—indignation, wit, and common sense are rarely so well braided—wrote in one of her letters that potatoes are a folk cure for arthritis. "You put one in yr. bra, and the arthritis simply vanishes," she wrote. It worked for her mother-in-law, at any rate. For Mitford, the news was "rather smashing." She wrote: "The potato hardly minds at all, one hopes."

* * *

"One of the secrets of a happy life," Iris Murdoch declared, "is continuous small treats." Thus, the brightness of aisle two, where the chips and the cookies reside. When I was a kid I loved Bugles, the trumpet-shaped corn chips. We'd put them on the ends of our fingers and pretend to be warlocks. In high school, a girlfriend saw me grazing from a bag and, casually blowing my mind, said, "Bugles taste like come."

I only rarely keep chips around because, like cereal, I'll polish them off. I wander this aisle, looking for more exotic offerings. I like the scene in *Monty Python's Life of Brian* where Brian is a food vendor at a gladiator tournament:

> BRIAN: Larks' tongues! Otters' noses! Ocelots' spleens!
> REG: Got any nuts?
> BRIAN: Haven't got any nuts, sorry. I've got wrens' livers, badgers' spleens . . .
> REG: No, no, no . . .
> BRIAN: Otters' noses?
> REG: I don't want any of that Roman rubbish!
> JUDITH: Why don't you sell proper food?
> BRIAN: Proper food?
> REG: Yeah, not those rich imperialist tidbits!
> BRIAN: Oh, don't blame me. I didn't ask to sell this stuff!
> REG: All right, bag of otters' noses, then.
> FRANCIS: Make it two.

America needs more exotic vending machines, as well. In some small French towns, you can buy a fresh baguette and good pizza from them. William Gibson, the author of *Neuromancer*, thinks we should emulate Japan: "Vending machines in Tokyo constitute a secret city of solitude," Gibson has written. "Limiting oneself to purchases from vending machines, it's possible to spend entire days in Tokyo without having to make eye contact with another sentient being."

When my kids where young, I kept gingersnaps in the house, selfishly, because it was a type of cookie they avoided. A box of any other kind would vanish instantly. A cookie and a glass of milk, after lunch, is a sure way to anchor yourself for a nap. Flannery O'Connor wrote in a journal, "Today I have proved myself a glutton—for Scotch oatmeal cookies and erotic thought. There is nothing left to say of me." O'Connor had big, beautiful, predatory teeth, with David Bowie cuspids, and I can imagine her not merely devouring cookies but picking the slivers of her enemies out with a toothpick. People are always offering me their homemade oatmeal cookies. In his very funny book *The Plagiarist in the Kitchen*, the English writer Jonathan Meades wrote that the notion of homemade made you wonder, "Whose home? Have you ever actually seen people's homes?"

\* \* \*

I swing into aisle three, the condiments aisle, pulling a U-turn wheelie. I come cart-to-cart with a big man, with gourmet jowls, who's studying the back of a tub of Hellmann's. "Mayonnaise" was one of Brautigan's favorite words; it's the last word in his cult classic, *Trout Fishing in America*. Here is an unlikely story but a true one: I was a founding volunteer at Burlington's nonprofit Brautigan Library, founded in 1990, that stocked only unpublished books, accepted without judgment. Richard Brautigan dreamed up a similar place in his novel *The Abortion*. In our library, writers sent in their manuscripts, and, for a token fee, we'd bind them and put them on shelves for visitors to browse. The bookends were mayonnaise jars. Almost no one came in. This gave me, when it was my turn to work the counter, time to eat sandwiches and raid the shelves. I'm sorry to report that no youthful Zadie Smithlings seemed to be hiding in those stacks. The Brautigan Library didn't survive into the internet era, which would have rendered it irrelevant in any case. During my final week as a volunteer, I was reading Thomas Hardy's *The Mayor of Casterbridge*. I finished it, blacked out the "r" in "Mayor" on the spine, and set the book on a shelf.

In the condiments aisle I can't help but recall my envy of the novelist Amy Bloom, who wrote that she keeps a second refrigerator in her kitchen, just for condiments. I'd fill half of my condiment fridge up with mustards. You don't have to have read Veblen to understand that if mustard were rare, we'd pay a fortune for it; there would be mustard societies, magazines, blind tastings. Robert Menasse's satirical, Brussels-based political novel, *The Capital*, is terrific, as I knew it would be when I read its first line: "Who invented mustard?" In his essay "Superman Comes to the Supermarket," Norman Mailer complained about the air in Los Angeles. "For an easterner there is never any salt in the wind," he wrote. He said it was like "Chinese egg rolls missing their mustard."

Heinz ketchup is a stalwart; it's as pandering as country radio. Growing up at the table, in American food writing, is often a story about slowly leaving ketchup behind. Calvin Trillin has recalled a tense moment when one of his daughters asked for ketchup for the first time. "How did you know about ketchup?" asks his wife, Alice. Trillin replies, "Those wild kids down the street probably told her . . . Maybe we oughtn't to let her play with them anymore." In her memoir *Hold Still*, Sally Mann describes the backlash she received after declaring about ketchup, in front of a *Times Magazine* writer, "It's common and I will not have common children." Years later, she still sounded shaken. "I was taken to task for the most self-mocking, flippant, two-glasses-of-red-wine-into-it comment *ever* about ketchup," she wrote. I put ketchup on three things: French fries, meatloaf, and breakfast hash, and I look forward to all three. I have a friend who dumps ketchup on his breakfast sandwiches; I avoid him until lunchtime. He's like the joker in one of Barry Hannah's short stories who puts ketchup on rice.

I'm running late. Just a few more things. The pickles are here, but not the ones I buy—Claussen, from the chilled aisle. Updike was a pickle guy. About New York City delis, he said, "A sandwich in one of those places usually has enough meat to feed three people. And all of those pickles. You know, there are pickle eaters and pickle refusers and I take what the refusers leave. I even steal other people's pickles." In a

1955 letter, James Beard wrote, "You know how queer I am for pickles." Benjamin Bradlee, the *Washington Post* editor, loved the inadvertently dirty headline that ran in his paper's food section, atop an article about canning: "You Can Put Pickles Up Yourself."

For some ineluctable reason, pickles and revenge tend to walk hand in hand. Both involve brine, perhaps. In *The Silence of the Lambs*, the novel and the film, a decapitated head is stuffed like a gefilte fish into a pickling jar. In the film *The Mask of Zorro*, Antonio Banderas, in a memorable scene, is forced to drink the brine in which his brother's head has been pickled. And in Guillermo Stitch's brave satirical novel *Lake of Urine*, a man keeps hundreds of jars of homemade pickles in his basement. He's proud of his stash. An enemy ruins every jar by placing a different note inside each one, enumerating the owner's many faults. The enemy reseals them all with glue.

In Salman Rushdie's novel *Midnight's Children*, pickling is an extended metaphor for both history and storytelling. Rushdie's narrator, Saleem Sinai, manages a pickle and chutney factory. He was born the moment India became independent after the partition. Saleem labels and stores each chapter he writes in a pickle jar, where he hopes his son may one day find them. He talks about his "chutnification of history." In the novel's last chapter, Saleem digresses at a key moment to contemplate the nature of pickling. "What is required for chutnification?" he asks. "Raw materials, obviously—fruit, vegetables, fish, vinegar, spices. Daily visits from Koli women with their saris hitched up between their legs. Cucumbers (like his nose, for instance), aubergines, mint." Rushdie reminds us that you can pickle almost anything. In his memoir, *My Cross to Bear*, Gregg Allman recalls the night Aretha Franklin dropped a five-gallon jug of pickled pigs' feet on a hotel lobby floor while wearing a mink coat.

*  *  *

Here in aisle four are salt, spices, tiers of oils, and hot sauce. I like salt so much that I nearly always salt my food before I taste it, and I've yet to regret it. My low blood pressure is one of the few healthy things about me. I became a fan of the late food writer Josh Ozersky when I read his burger recipe. "Season it liberally with salt," Ozersky wrote, "and when I say liberally, I mean like Noam Chomsky." Chefs hate it when you ask your server for salt. Cree and I once asked for salt in one of the chef Wylie Dufresne's post-WD-50 restaurants in lower Manhattan. The man himself stomped out of the kitchen to get a look at us. We really saw the hostility at work beneath the bonhomie. What could we say? His food needed salt.

In *Table Manners*, his etiquette book, the West Coast chef Jeremiah Tower writes about the use of salt and pepper in restaurants. "If brilliant, the chef will [dispense salt and pepper] the second before the food leaves the kitchen. If not, it's up to you to get over any issues about insulting the chef. You are the one paying. Ask for salt and pepper mills." According to Eugene Walter, Truman Capote got revenge on a waitress who offended him by loosening the top of every saltshaker in a restaurant's dining room. When I use black pepper out of a shaker, in a diner, I unscrew the top first and pour some into the palm of my hand. That's how you can get at pepper unimpeded; you can get as much as you really want. According to kitchen lore, black pepper pressed into a fresh cut will stop it from bleeding—something I've never tried.

"We taste the salt from ourselves, which is the tastiest salt there is," Chang-rae Lee wrote in his novel *My Year Abroad*. One of the great things is a radish, run around in good butter and salt. One day Cree came back from a run and rubbed a radish across the salt that had dried on her chest and then ate it—a sexy move. We like to keep salt in small bowls, for easy access, not in shakers or the spice cabinet. You don't want to have the sort of kitchen Anne Tyler describes, in *The Accidental Tourist*, that is "so completely alphabetized, you'd find the allspice next to the ant poison." Updike was Tyler's biggest fan but, in a *New Yorker* review, he dinged Tyler for that line, finding it implausible.

Spices can be found near the outmoded "international" sections in most grocery stores. These sections have gotten better; we'll know they've become great when the designation is retired entirely. One of the best things about being alive these past few decades, as an eater and as a reader, is the expansion of the American palate and the expansion of the history and literature about that palate. It's literature about immigrants trying to recover through food what they've lost by circumstance. It's about the inclusion of traditional outsiders such as women, people of color, and cooks of partial education.

Jhumpa Lahiri has written exactingly about what it was like to grow up in Rhode Island with Bengali parents who were homesick for the foods of their youth. Lahiri's father had a big "food suitcase" he'd take back home with him on visits. He'd spend days shopping, slowly filling it. "Into the suitcase went an arsenal of lentils and every conceivable spice, wrapped in layers of cloth ripped from an old sari and stitched into individual pockets," Lahiri wrote. "In went white poppy seeds, resin made from date syrup, and as many tins of Ganesh mustard oil as possible. In went Lapchu tea, to be brewed only on special occasions, and sacks of black-skinned Gobindovog rice, so named, it is said, because it's fit for offering to the god Govinda. In went six kinds of *dalmoot*, a salty, crunchy snack mix bought from big glass jars in a tiny store at the corner of Vivekananda Road and Cornwallis Street." Her prose, at its best, is always this incantatory. Sometimes fresh fruit, illegal to import, was tucked inside. One year Lahiri's grandmother found a *parval*, a squash-like vegetable, inside the suitcase, and she wept.

Lahiri's parents would envy the big new "Indo-Pak grocery" that opens in a strip mall near Milwaukee in Ayad Akhtar's novel *Homeland Elegies*. "It was astonishing to me," Akhtar writes, "that there were enough of us now in the area to justify the new grocery store's generous square footage, its aisles and aisles of packaged naans and dals and sacks of basmati, the masalas, the pakora mixes, the biryani mixes, the dazzling mounds of cayenne and turmeric and ground cardamom, the tins of ghee and bottles of bitter pickle, the rows of fresh mint, coriander, methi, of our native fruits—mangoes, guavas, lychees, Punjabi kinu." *Homeland Elegies* is a meditation on the possibilities and limitations of American life, and the food writing in it casually underscores Akhtar's themes.

Michelle Zauner's memoir, *Crying in H Mart*, is in part a soulful paean to that Korean American supermarket chain. H Marts are enormous. They're where, Zauner writes, "parachute kids flock to find the brand of instant noodles that reminds them of home," and "where Korean families buy rice cakes to make tteokguk, the beef and rice cake soup that brings in the New Year. It's the only place where you can find a giant vat of peeled garlic, because it's the only place that truly understands how much garlic you'll need for the kind of food your people eat." In the 1980s and '90s, "Kmart realism"—bleak, spare fiction, set in laundromats and third-rate motels—was a genre of the moment. H Mart realism, as we might call it, is bringing a similar kind of news.

\* \* \*

"There is no editor," Ezra Pound wrote, "whom I wouldn't cheerfully fry in oil." Pound spent many years in Italy; he would surely have fried up that editor in olive oil. Once a year or so I taste an olive oil that makes me want to devote time to chasing down the ineffable ones. Day in and day out, we make do with the extra-virgin from California Olive Ranch, which is affordable and widely available. I'm mostly in agreement with the narrator of James Hamilton-Paterson's witty novel *Cooking with Fernet Branca*, who thought that "olive oil snobs are even worse than wine snobs." My favorite bit in *Cooking with Fernet Branca* is when Hamilton-Paterson's narrator tries to convince us to shell and clean two dozen fresh mussels, roll them in finely grated dark chocolate, and deep-fry them in rosemary-scented olive oil. I'd watch a TikTok of someone attempting this.

I graduated from Middlebury but never attended the Bread Loaf Writers' Conference, founded in 1920 and held up the mountain each summer, near the site of Robert Frost's cabin. Game-changing gossip came out of Bread Loaf. I was reminded of one story while reading *Blood, Bone, and Marrow*, Ted Geltner's biography of Harry Crews. Crews taught at Bread Loaf in 1970, and one night he fell into conversation with a group that included Avis DeVoto, Julia Child's friend. Crews thought DeVoto was uptight, and he decided to loosen the mood. "What we ought to do here sometime is work out all our old frustrations and hostilities and all that," Crews said. "What we need to do is have a Mazola party."

DeVoto took his bait. "What's a Mazola party?" she asked. "Well," Crews replied, happily, "you get a room that has tile floor, preferably, and you get about thirteen men and twelve women, or thirteen women and twelve men, and everybody takes their clothes off. And then everybody just pours Mazola oil all over themselves, just rubs it all around. And then you just rub and hug and slither around there with everybody's bodies, and I'm telling you, it just gets out all those old frustrations and fears. And you come out feeling great." There was total silence, until the room broke out in laughter.

When did people stop collecting bacon grease in coffee cans? Nanny kept cans in the backs of her refrigerators, ready for frying. It's a thrifty habit that needs a comeback. But then, as Montaigne asked, *Que sçay-je*—what do I know?

\* \* \*

Hillary Clinton, when she was first lady, is said to have kept more than a hundred varieties of hot sauce in the White House. She also eats raw jalapeños like potato chips, according to a former aide, because she finds them "refreshing." These facts should have been part of her campaign slogans. Today I'm idling in front of this market's meager selection of hot sauces. At home we keep eight or ten different bottles, but most of them gather dust. We settled a long time ago on Marie Sharp's from Belize. Its heat is on point, and it isn't acidic or vinegary. It's rarely in supermarkets, so we order it in bulk to have extras to hand out. Eugene Walter wanted a water pistol filled with Tabasco to aim at cops. The critic Clive James accidentally ingested a hot pepper while eating with Didion and her husband, John Gregory Dunne, in Los Angeles. "I enjoyed their company very much and did my best not to let them know I had swallowed a habanero," he wrote later. "They probably thought my muffled sobs were due to homesickness."

I used to drive five hours each way from Manhattan to Cambridge, Massachusetts, to attend the annual "Hell Night" at Chris Schlesinger's much-missed restaurant, East Coast Grill. Hell Night came about because Schlesinger got tired of customers complaining, when he put a fiery dish on his menu, that it wasn't hot enough. So once a year he decided to really go for it. On Hell Night, the air inside East Coast Grill was so *picante* that some of the chefs breathed through gas masks. The heat of the dishes, in long sequence, made me numb. I felt I'd been zapped by mutant radiation, like in a 1950s horror movie. When you were clearly really suffering, young servers, in the manner of 1940s cigarette girls, would come by with the antidote: they'd hand you a Creamsicle. Once a year, in November, when our kids and their friends are around for Thanksgiving, we honor Schlesinger by staging our own Hell Night. It's a cruel-to-be-kind sort of adventure.

I take a bottle of fish sauce from the shelf. This pungent condiment, made from krill that have been salted and left to ferment, was given its rapturous due by Viet Thanh Nguyen in *The Sympathizer*. "How we longed for the grand cru of Phu Quoc Island and its vats brimming with the finest vintage of pressed anchovies!" he wrote. "We used fish sauce the way Transylvanian villagers wore cloves of garlic to ward off vampires, in our case to establish a perimeter with those Westerners who could never understand that what was truly fishy was the nauseating stench of cheese. What was fermented fish compared to curdled milk?" People become sauce addicts. Betty Fussell wrote that even though Kingsley Amis's second wife, Elizabeth Jane Howard, was an excellent cook, he insisted on always having a bottle of HP Sauce—named after London's Houses of Parliament—at the table with him. No matter the menu, he used it "at full tilt." Howard was routinely horrified.

\* \* \*

I push into aisle five, where beans, pasta, and rice lurk. "Life should be a beano," W. B. Yeats said. He wasn't talking about the anti-flatulence pills. Yeats meant a noisy celebration. Gregg Allman, in his memoir, describes getting laid for the first time as "the finest thing I'd had since black-eyed peas."

In Les Blank's documentary *A Poem Is a Naked Person*, Leon Russell eats a plate of rice and beans onstage, at his piano. He's almost as happy as I've seen a person look. The happiest I've seen a person look is Ronnie Hawkins, in *The Last Waltz*, singing "Who Do You Love?" with the Band.

Southern writers take beans as seriously as they take biscuits. In Carson McCullers's novel *The Member of the Wedding*, a woman requests that, when she dies, a plate of Hoppin' John be waved under her nose, just to make sure she's really gone. Eugene Walter wrote about a lavish meal at the Grand Véfour in Paris with William Faulkner and Katherine Anne Porter. French publishers were paying. Afterward, as they were all sipping their "1870 cognac or Grand Marnier or whatever," Porter commented, "Back home, first butter beans'll be coming in." Faulkner replied, wistfully, "The baby speckled ones."

The influence of beans on Southern driving habits may require scholarly attention. In her memoir, *The Yellow House*, the New Orleans writer Sarah M. Broom describes teaching her mother to drive by using the lid of a red beans pot as the steering wheel. In her poem "Frame," Robin Coste Lewis recalls practicing driving at twelve: "My majorette's baton became the stick shift, / cans of butter beans the brake, gas, and clutch." You know you've mastered the stick shift, I discovered while young, when you can eat a plate of rice and beans that's on your lap while driving in traffic.

Red beans and rice is the traditional Monday meal in Louisiana. Monday was wash day; women would put on beans to simmer while they worked. A hambone from last night's dinner imparted flavor. The point was that a pot of beans, cooking slowly, freed you up. Or so I thought until I read the Puerto Rico–born poet Judith Ortiz Cofer's poem "Beans: An Apologia for Not Loving to Cook." In Cofer's poem, "the cloying smell of boiling beans" simply means waiting, "for wars, affairs, periods / of grieving, the rains, *el mal tiempo*." She grew to hate them, because

> *. . . The mothers turned hard*
> *at the stove, resisting our calls with the ultimate*
> *  threat of*
> *burned beans. The vigil made them statues, rivulets*
> *of sweat coursing down their faces, pooling at their*
> *  collarbones.*
> *They turned hard away from our demands for atten-*
> *  tion and love.*

This might be the place to mention that the best bean stew I'm aware of is tucked away in one of Schlesinger's books, written with John Willoughby, called *How to Cook Meat*. Its full title is Lamb, Leek, and White Bean Stew with Oregano, Walnuts, and Hard Cheese. Use homemade stock if you can. The aroma will temporarily increase the value of your house by thirty thousand dollars. You can thank me later. Simmer your own beans rather than buying canned, while keeping in mind Vertamae Smart-Grosvenor's advice (she was speaking of cowpeas): "Remove all the peas that look weird."

\*   \*   \*

Frank Sinatra, served an imperfect bowl of pasta in a restaurant, once stood up and smashed the offending dish into a wall. What it is about pasta that makes people want to heave it around? Richard Brautigan threw dinner parties at his house in Montana; the food fights that resulted were so intense that the interiors frequently had to be repainted. At one dinner, Brautigan felt so harangued by his wife that he took a serving bowl of spaghetti and dumped it over his own head. Then he silently returned the bowl to the center of the table. "He's sitting there quietly continuing to eat with his head covered with spaghetti," recalled Robert Creeley's wife, Bobbie. "It was dripping down his face and onto his shoulders like a wig."

The novelist Elaine Dundy, Kenneth Tynan's wife, showed up one night at the apartment of her friend the writer Judy Feiffer, with her dress covered in spaghetti. "Ken and I disagreed about a play," she explained.* The Velvet Underground's Nico, according to her biographer, made a pot of spaghetti with extra anchovies along with her boyfriend on the day Prince Charles married Diana in 1981. They took two tabs of acid each, on top of heroin, and wallpapered their apartment with the sauce so that the place stank for a month.

Crucial pasta advice comes from Calvin Trillin. His rule of thumb in a restaurant is that "a pasta dish is likely to be satisfying in inverse proportion to the number of ingredients that the menu lists as being in it." Have good meatballs, John

---

* Woe to those who disagreed with Tynan about theater. "I doubt if I could love anyone who did not wish to see *Look Back in Anger*," he wrote about John Osborne's 1956 play.

Thorne wrote, because, "What is a meatball, after all, if not a triumph of quick wit over brute reality?"

When we were just married and living in Brooklyn, our go-to dinner was pasta puttanesca, served to anyone who came over. It was cheap; it required one pot, one pan, and items we had in the pantry anyway: anchovies, garlic, black olives, capers, canned tuna, maybe a tomato, and a torn-up sardine. For dessert we usually served lemon ice cream, no machine required, from John Thorne's book *Outlaw Cook*. I still make it every summer.

Cree's dad, Bruce, referred to pasta dishes that were made up on the spot, from whatever was in the house, as *pasta nada*—pasta from nothing. What's for dinner, Bruce? Often enough it was a baguette, a bottle of red, and pasta nada. Someone should steal that for a book title.

I don't need a box of mac and cheese, but here they are. Annie's or Kraft? Cree is in the former camp; I'm in the latter. Either way, I double underlined this sentence in Quentin Tarantino's novelization of *Once Upon a Time in Hollywood*: "The directions say to add milk and butter, but Cliff thinks if you can afford to add milk and butter you can afford to eat something else." I'm not buying rice today, but a sentence from Ocean Vuong, in *On Earth We're Briefly Gorgeous*, will remind you not to waste food. The narrator's parents told him: "Every grain of rice you leave behind is one maggot you eat in hell."

\* \* \*

I swerve into the baking aisle for a can of sweetened condensed milk. The Jewish-Hungarian chef George Lang (1924–2011), in his memoir *Nobody Knows the Truffles I've Seen*, tells you what to do with it. Remove the label and boil the can gently for two and a half hours, replacing the water in the pot as it evaporates. You end up with a dense, creamy, caramel *doce de leite*. Spooned on top of ice cream, it's a no-fuss dessert of the gods. Or, as I have sometimes done, you can take the can into bed with you, along with a spoon.

* * *

I sweep my cart along the back of the store to cruise the sausages. According to the historian Paul Johnson, Heidegger is recorded to have laughed only once, at a picnic with Ernst Jünger in the Harz Mountains. "Jünger leaned over to pick up a sauerkraut and sausage roll," Johnson writes, "and his lederhosen split with a tremendous crack." Charles Simic is our sausage poet. "Even their names," he's written, "are poetry to me: chorizo, merguez, rosette, boudin noir, kielbasa, luganega, cotechino, zampone, chipolata, linguiça, weisswurst." When it comes to cooking them, it took me years to learn, there is only one thing that matters—that you cook them slowly, thirty to forty minutes in the pan, so that they become sticky with ooze.

Not far away is the glum seafood section. Nonetheless, I grab a combo-pack of supermarket sushi, a favorite snack. Back home, we'll fall upon it, eating it standing up in the kitchen, as if it were fresh mozzarella or a ripe peach. Before I leave the seafood counter, I should mention Robert Hughes's thought experiment in his book *A Jerk on One End*, which has stuck with me. What would it be like, he wondered, if fish and angler were reversed? Here is Hughes, and he makes you feel it all:

It is a bright, breezy May day and you are strolling along one of the piers at Malibu. You stop at a vendor's cart and buy a hot dog with mustard and relish. You lean on the railing and take a first bite. Suddenly your gullet is convulsed with a choking pain and a sharp pull snaps your head forward and down. Something hard, sharp, and metallic is stuck in your throat. The shock is completely outside your experience. In an effort to resist it, you run frantically back and forth on the pier, but the pressure is inexorable, and your lungs have begun to fill with blood. Over the side you go, and hit the water wildly struggling. The unidentifiable force drags you down. On the bed of the bay, something enormous and unknown grabs you and, if you are lucky, kills you with a blow to the back of the head.

Hughes was a brilliant food writer. His long introduction to *The Balthazar Cookbook*, which follows that restaurant's ingredients back to their sources, is a serious pleasure.

\* \* \*

I need only one more thing today: a chicken to roast for dinner. The most honest, if difficult, way to procure one is to raise it yourself. We didn't kill many of the chickens we kept in Garrison. They were layers, not meat birds, and any-way, other animals—coyotes, skunks, hawks, weasels—did enough killing. They'd steal into the coop at night like Ted Bundy into a dormitory. We did make a meal of one of our roosters, because it kept attacking Hattie, who was then seven or eight. These attacks were funny at the start. The rooster was a charming, self-satisfied grump, a Foghorn Leg-horn with an easily wounded ego. He charged at everyone as if they'd insulted his wattle, but he always backed off at the last second. But one afternoon he got Hattie on the ground, his wings flapping, and that was it. His beak was at her eye level.

So we found a hammer and two long nails. We drove the nails into a stump's flat top, three inches apart. Cree caught him, pinning him in a fenced-in corner. She held him up as if he were a prize pumpkin. He was furious. "Sorry, old fella," she said. We stretched his head between the nails. Cree held him down and pulled up his neck feathers, exposing the neck it-self. Exposed, a chicken's neck is thinner and more vulner-able than you might expect. I had the easy job. A *thwack* with the axe, and it was over. There was a gush of vermilion. Cree let go. The headless body, all chest, like a football stud charging through paper, ran in a long and tilted arc, strew-ing blood. It was as if he'd been a balloon, end held between pinched fingers, that was let go. After three long seconds of motoring, he fell over in the grass.

Cree loved our chickens and put a lot of time and effort into their care. She was distraught every time one was killed over-night. But this rooster had been her determined foe. After he was dead, we boiled water, using the outdoor rig we used for boiling crabs and frying turkeys. We dunked the bird in the water, scalding him, then plucked his feathers and gutted him. Cree made sure to pluck out the heart, which she fried with butter and salt and immediately ate. She had her revenge, and it was delicious. We fried up the liver, too.* The rooster became a Tuesday night coq au vin.

There are a lot of stories, in the literature of chicken-killing, about the process going badly. The poet Kevin Young wrote,

> *Some nights dinner would just get up*
> *& run off because I hadn't wrung it right.*

It's worth knowing how to kill a chicken. This is made apparent in the playwright David Hare's memoir, *The Blue Touch Paper*. While Hare was courting Margaret Matheson, the woman who'd become his first wife, he visited her family in the English countryside. Her father, "as some sort of initiation rite," asked him to do him a favor and kill eleven chickens. "I was determined not to be fazed," Hare wrote. He went out into the driving rain and wrung their necks, one by one.

Barbara Pym, in her novel *Excellent Women*, writes about a woman who is convinced that birds are taking over the planet. She tells her son, "I eat as many birds as possible . . . I have them sent from Harrods or Fortnum's, and sometimes

---

* "Have you ever considered what a triumph of civilization it is to be able to buy a pound of chicken livers?" the essayist Phyllis Rose asked. "If you lived on a farm and had to kill a chicken when you wanted to eat one, you wouldn't ever accumulate a pound of chicken livers."

I go and look at them in the cold meats department. They do them up very prettily with aspic jelly and decorations." She adds, "At least we can eat our enemies." A lot of pale chicken is consumed in Pym's fiction. In *Some Tame Gazelle*, boiled chicken is served to religious men because, a bit like them, the meal is cold, white, and muffled with sauce.

Cree doesn't eat white meat, except under duress. She's the author of the only cookbook I'm aware of (*Poulet*, from 2011) that doesn't contain a single recipe for breast meat. To her, breast is dullsville. We fight about the doneness of chicken. She likes hers on the rare side, even a bit pink at the bone. This drives me insane. I'm with Pearl Bailey, who wrote in *Pearl's Kitchen*, "Nothing destroys me more than raw chicken." In Toni Morrison's *Song of Solomon*, a husband tastes his supper and delivers this devastating verdict: "Your chicken is red at the bone." That comment wouldn't hurt Cree's feelings at all. She lives for the thighs. These used to be hard to find in America, especially in restaurants. "What Have We Done with the Thighs?" Jim Harrison asked in the early nineties. He'd discovered that American producers shipped most of them to Russia because Americans preferred breast. "Chicken breasts are the moral equivalent of a TV commercial," he wrote. "Sixty percent of those under thirty in America have never seen a live chicken and couldn't tell a thigh from Jon Bon Jovi's chin."

If you've read Deborah Levy's thorny novels, you might remember the scene in *The Cost of Living* in which her narrator bicycles home with a chicken in her bag. The bag rips open, the chicken falls out, and a car immediately runs over it, flattening it. Levy genially serves it for dinner anyway. Extreme spatchcocking! Levy's chicken resembles one Jason Epstein prepared at Norman Mailer's house in Provincetown. Epstein wrote about it in *Eating*, his memoir. He butterflied a few chickens to make chicken under a brick. "If it all goes well the chickens will emerge from the process looking like lacquered roadkill," he wrote, "a chicken pancake with the curve of the legs and thighs a mere tracery against the crisp skin of the flattened breasts." That line—"a chicken pancake"—I find aspirational. I'm not sure I've ever had a chicken pancake.

I find aspirational, too, the poet Thom Gunn's method for roasting chicken. "The secret of a perfect chicken is obvious, though it took me a while to learn it," he wrote to his two octogenarian aunts in the late 1990s. "You baste with butter every ten minutes, so how can anybody fail when what you end up with is chicken meat soaked with butter?" The editors of Gunn's letters note that his aunts' response does not survive.

I consider making fried chicken tonight, but it's real work. What you want is someone who knows what they're doing to cook it for you. The soprano Leontyne Price was born in Laurel, Mississippi. Eugene Walter described her as "one of those who fried chicken in a way that you thought it flew in, dropped its feathers outside the window, and jumped into the grease. Because there was no grease. Crunch and succulent, crunch and succulent, crunch and succulent." The sportswriter Dan Jenkins, in his memoir, wrote about the importance of not trying to hide fried chicken's decadence by serving it with, say, a salad. He wanted nothing "fernlike," he wrote, next to his fried chicken.

In one of his poems, Jack Gilbert recalls sleeping with a woman whose name he can no longer remember. He remembers not just "how strong / her thighs were" but how she tore apart

> the barbecued chicken with her hands,
> and wiped the grease on her breasts.

I take a five-pound Perdue organic chicken. I know what I'm going to do with it. Bruce Jay Friedman said the way to learn to cook is to pick up one tip from every person you date. The first kitchen tip I ever learned from Cree was this: slip a large handful of herbs, even if it's just parsley, into a chicken's cavity before cooking. This adds flavor, but it also makes the chicken look wonderful when you pull it from the oven. (Also, slip several pats of butter under the skin.) Nearly thirty years later, it's a weekly dinner.

I'm done shopping. I push my cart toward the checkout line, snagging a baguette on the fly. In the old days, waiting in line, I'd scan the tabloid racks and flip through a copy of the *National Enquirer* to see who had six months to live and whose plastic surgery was sagging. "Everything we need that is not food or love is here in the tabloid racks," DeLillo wrote in *White Noise*. "The tales of the supernatural and the extraterrestrial. The miracle vitamins, the cures for cancer, the remedies for obesity. The cults of the famous and the dead." Now I'll read Twitter, or the *Times*, on my phone while waiting, or I'll use the self-checkout machines. I screw up on these while weighing my produce and give the machine the finger. I look like a madman. I take my bags out to my car and drive home.

It's possible I'll be back an hour later. I like to read in supermarket parking lots. Being a working book critic means that, some days, I'll need to read six or seven hours at a stretch. Nice work if you can get it, but try it—stamina is required. If I climb into a comfortable chair I'll soon be snoozing, no matter how good the book is, so I avoid comfortable chairs. To keep alert, I move around. I'll read in a coffee shop, then a library, then a different coffee shop. Leaving a coffee shop, I'll climb into the car and drive to the ocean and read in the front seat, propping the book on the steering wheel. Then I'll drive to a grocery store parking lot and, between chapters, watch the people emerge, blinking like voles, into the sunlight. Here is life's rich pageant. For people-watching, it's better than the Met Gala red carpet.

# INTERLUDE:
# A SWIM,
# OR A NAP

Go to bed; tired is stupid.

—**URSULA K. LE GUIN**, *A Wizard of Earthsea*

When I was a teenager, I hadn't yet read John Cheever's short story "The Swimmer," but I'd lived it in my own nocturnal, vaguely criminal sort of way. Maybe you know "The Swimmer," or have seen the film with Burt Lancaster. It's about a man named Neddy Merrill who realizes, at an afternoon cocktail party, that he might be able to "swim home"—some eight miles, hopping in and out of the pools of friends. "The day was beautiful," Cheever wrote, "and it seemed to him that a long swim might enlarge and celebrate its beauty."

The swim starts promisingly. Along the way there are cocktails to consume, friends to embrace, old lovers who might be glad to see him. A few of his portages while in swim trunks, across highways and through horse farms, are embarrassing, but nothing he can't handle. As Neddy moves along, we begin to realize his mind has come unstitched. He's lost everything that mattered to him. "The Swimmer" is a story I relish, in part, for its hymns to swimming, life's best activity that doesn't take place in the bedroom or kitchen. I am beside Neddy when he thinks, "That he lived in a world so generously supplied with water seemed like a clemency, a beneficence."

There's no verb for traveling while hopping from swimming pool to swimming pool. Perhaps "cheevering" would suffice. During the summers of my youth, late at night, my friends and I would cheever through my neighborhood. Nearly every house had a rectangular or kidney-shaped pool out back. We'd make a circuit of dozens of these pools—quietly unlatching the screen doors, swimming from end to end in the dark, then tiptoeing out the screen doors on the other side. We could do this for hours. If girls were along, we might pause to make out a little. Maybe someone had a six-pack of beer. We tried not to make noise. This was not yet the National Rifle Association's America. We were more worried about being chased away than being gutshot by a Fox News nut. On one memorable humid August night, the joke was on us. The neighbors a few houses down had moved to a retirement home. Their house was shuttered. The pool cleaners had stopped coming. Over the course of many months the unattended pool had turned into a fetid swamp, thick with weeds and muck. In the dark, we had no way of knowing. I leapt in first and hit the water with a *thurk*. It was as if I'd fallen into a moat filled with deliquescing bodies. Before I could cry out, I heard the *thurks* of my friends around me. We scrambled out, retching, and scraped off the ooze.

This misadventure aside, I knew the following to be true: any day I can swim is a good day. On summer evenings, when we were raising our kids in New Jersey, Cree and I would walk down to the Delaware River, about a block from our house, and float in the cool eddies, looking at birds and turtles. Other afternoons, I drove to a YMCA to swim. Some people don't like the smell of chlorine on their bodies. I do, maybe because it reminds me of being a kid. I don't always shower afterward. I keep swim trunks and a towel in the back seat of my car, the way a teenage boy carries a condom in his wallet. You never know when an opportunity might present itself. About an hour from where we lived there was a Russian bathhouse. It was a treat to pop in there and soak like a foreign dignitary, moving between hot pools and cold ones. Dunk your head under the water; you've got your own quiet down there. Iris Murdoch wrote memorably about water; her novels are filled with lakes and rivers and spas. "Swimming, like dying, seems to solve all problems," she wrote, "and you remain alive."

On a hot spring day a few years ago, I set out to see if I could cheever my way up the West Side of Manhattan. My editors at *Esquire*, where I had a column, were happiness facilitators when they weren't darkening my door about deadlines. They helped me get into some pools that aren't normally open to civilians (or non–hotel guests). That morning, I put swim trunks, a towel, goggles, and a book into a small bag, and set off. It felt strange, traveling toward a swimming pool in a subway. It reminded me of being on the Metro in Oslo, where the final stop drops you off in the woods. I spent my morning at the rooftop pool of the Gansevoort, a luxury hotel in the Meatpacking District. Up there you get a wide-angle view of lower Manhattan and the new Whitney Museum. The view from the Gansevoort poolside was nearly as sleek: the place was packed with tanned hard bodies. I sank into the aqua blue pool and floated until I felt like William Hurt in *Altered States*. I did not have a tan or defined abs. All of a sudden, as if my psyche had ordered them from room service, two plus-size female models began to pose around the pool for a female photographer. I felt better about myself instantly.

I made my way up to midtown and spent the early afternoon in the basement-level pool in the Chatwal, a hotel not far from Bryant Park. Here there was New Age music and a sense of Zen, primeval calm. I can imagine Bill Murray, in a Manhattan remake of *Lost in Translation*, having a well-appointed spiritual crisis down there. I was alone. I swam against the current of the powerful lap pool until I was tired. I soaked in the hot tub, the surface of the water fizzing like the top of a glass of champagne, or like the citrus oil that leaps from a clementine as you peel it. I'd been in the water for three or four hours today; the tips of my fingers were wrinkled. I toweled off and, like Neddy, kept moving. I made my way to the Upper West Side, where I swam in the deep blue pool on the eighteenth floor of the Mandarin Oriental hotel. The room had stone walls and vaulted ceilings. I paddled about in this uncommonly beautiful pool as the sunset began to spread its way over the Hudson River.

My perfect day was nearing its end. I doubled back downtown and had dinner with a friend on the roof of the Hotel Americano, in Chelsea. I was tempted to leap into the small pool up there, lit by underwater lights, but no one else was soaking, so I went to my table. The martinis up there taste good; the Mexican food better. I felt I could almost see my house out across the horizon, the way that Neddy, in Cheever's story, sensed, "with a cartographer's eye, that string of swimming pools, that quasi-subterranean stream that curved across the country." Cheever made this stream of pools sound as happy as one of Jack Kerouac's western highways. I began to wonder if I could swim home.

Almost every afternoon, I take a swim (which induces hunger) or a nap. The former is more invigorating, but the latter is easier to pull off.

Naps have a bad reputation in America, where sleep deprivation is worn like a merit badge. We know more now about sleep in general and about how napping in particular improves the memory and clears the mind. Dire things happen when you're sleep-deprived. The helmsman of the *Exxon Valdez* ran it aground, the NTSB said, because of "fatigue and excessive workload."

The laureate of the nap, in the Western world at any rate, is Winston Churchill. Not for him the twenty-minute, head-on-desk doze. Here is what he said, in one of his greatest utterances: "You must sleep sometime between lunch and dinner, and no halfway measures. Take off your clothes and get into bed. That's what I always do. Don't think you will be doing less work because you sleep during the day. That's a foolish notion held by people who have no imaginations. You will be able to accomplish more. You get two days in one—well, at least one and a half." I've lived by these words for at least two decades.

There are some refinements of which you should be aware. The first is: wake up early every day and put in five or six hours of committed work. It's easier to perform this kind of labor when you know a reward is coming. You will need a cold, quiet room. Now take off your clothes (my wife calls these "pants-off naps") and climb in. A steep part of the pleasure for me is reading on my phone for thirty minutes or so before I go to sleep, catching up on news and the yack on my Twitter feed. I'll play a game or two on a backgammon app I like. Upon waking, there are still mistakes the rookie can make. The first of these is to omit taking a shower. To properly jump-start your second day, you need to blast away the cobwebs. You can even put on fresh clothes. The second common mistake is to let postnap guilt sour your mood. Prevent this by getting back to your desk for a few solid hours.

Philip Roth came around to the siesta. "Let me tell you about the nap," he said on National Public Radio, laughing. "It's absolutely fantastic. When I was a kid, my father was always trying to tell me how to be a man, and he said to me, I was maybe nine, and he said to me, 'Philip, whenever you take a nap, take your clothes off, put a blanket on you, and you're going to sleep better.' Well, as with everything, he was right . . . Then the best part of it is that when you wake up, for the first fifteen seconds, you have no idea where you are. You're just alive. That's all you know. And it's bliss, it's absolute bliss."

# 4

# DRINKING

Baby, why aren't we drunk?

—**CHELSEY MINNIS**, *Baby, I Don't Care*

I make a martini, Gordon's or Barr Hill, every night at seven with, in my mind at least, a matador's formality. I use dense, square ice cubes. Like the *pop* of a cork exiting a bottle, a martini's being shaken is one of civilization's indispensable sounds. The martini is the only American invention, Mencken wrote, as perfect as a sonnet.

I like my martinis shaken rather than stirred because they seem colder and because the ice crystals that swim briefly on the surface are ethereal. I also like mine *extremely* dry. I was pleased to read, in the 2018 *Times* obituary of Tommy Rowles, the longtime bartender at Bemelmans Bar at the Carlyle hotel, that his secret was to omit vermouth entirely. "A bottle of vermouth," he said, "you should just open it and look at it." Modern cocktail orthodoxy is not kind to me, or to Tommy. Stirring, these days, is in, and vermouth is poured with a heavy hand. T. S. Eliot would not have minded. He was a vermouth man, so much so that he named one of his cats Noilly Prat, after his favorite brand. When I do add vermouth I apply Hemingway's formula, 15:1, in honor of Field Marshal Bernard Montgomery, who liked gin to outnumber vermouth in the same ratio he wanted to outnumber opponents in battle. The toast I make, with whoever is present, is usually the one I learned from the late Caroline Herron, a former editor at the *Times Book Review*: "To the confusion of our enemies." The toast Jack Nicholson makes in *Easy Rider*—"To old D. H. Lawrence"—isn't bad, either.

"The world and its martinis are mine!" Patricia Highsmith exclaimed in her diaries. Martinis inspire this sort of enthusiasm. Frederick Seidel, in his poem "At Gracie Mansion," refers to an ice-cold martini as a "see-through on a stem." The poet Richard Wilbur liked to add "fennel juice and foliage" to his. I'd like to be like Eloise, in the children's book by Kay Thompson, and keep a bottle of gin in my bedroom. If you want to go broke quickly rather than slowly, drink your martinis outside the house.

Occasionally I'll mix a vodka martini, recalling that Langston Hughes appeared in a Smirnoff advertisement. Vodka martinis flush out the snobs, who don't consider them martinis at all. Roger Angell, whose *New Yorker* essay "Dry Martini" is the best thing I've read on the subject, admitted that he and his wife moved from gin to vodka because vodka was "less argumentative." The best paean to the vodka martini appears in Lawrence Osborne's amazing book *The Wet and the Dry*, which is about trying to get a drink in countries where to do so is against the law. Osborne decides that, with its olive, his vodka martini tastes like "cold seawater at the bottom of an oyster."

Don't get all excited, as did Kenneth Tynan, and try to take your vodka martini rectally. Tynan had read, in Alan Watts's autobiography, that this was a good idea. Tynan had his girlfriend inject the contents of a large wineglass of vodka, via an enema tube, into his rectum. "Within ten minutes the agony is indescribable," he wrote in his diary. His anus became "tightly compressed" and blood seeped from it. It took three days for the pain to abate. "Oh, the perils of hedonism!" he wrote.

I make my first drink on the late side because I like it too much. I also want to prolong the anticipation. Alcohol is, as Benjamin Franklin noticed, constant proof that God loves us. I drink more than most people but less than some. I don't have an especially big tank; my tolerance is not Homeric. But almost nightly I drink two martinis and, with dinner, a glass or two of wine, without negative effects in the morning. If I have that third glass of wine, my morning at the desk becomes an afternoon at the desk.

Drinking alone doesn't depress me, the way it does some people. Franklin didn't recommend it. "He that drinks his cider alone, let him catch his horse alone," he wrote. But Christopher Hitchens said that solo drinks "can be the happiest glasses you ever drain," and Norman Mailer, in his novel *Tough Guys Don't Dance*, praised what he called "that impregnable hauteur which is, perhaps, the most satisfying aspect of solitary drinking." When alone, I'll put on good loud music, of the sort Cree does not especially like (jazz or Hüsker Dü) and read magazines and eat cheese until I get tiddly and head for bed. But I prefer companions. When I learn that someone new is coming over, I mentally ask the same questions Kingsley Amis did: "Does he drink? Is he jolly?" Alcohol can bring out the poetry in a person's soul.

In 2006, Gary Shteyngart, the irrepressible author of novels such as *The Russian Debutante's Handbook* and *Super Sad True Love Story*, gave an interview to the Denver-based magazine *Modern Drunkard*. It's one of the great interviews of the new century and some enterprising young editor should print it as a chapbook. In the meantime, find it online and send the link to your friends. James Baldwin may have said, "I don't know any writers who don't drink," but that was a long time ago. Shteyngart's complaint is that writers don't belly up to the bar with the enthusiasm they once did. "We're this sterilized profession, we all know our Amazon.com rankings to the nearest digit," he said. "The literary community is not backing me up here. I'm all alone." He added, "It's so pathetic when I think about my ancestors. Give them a bottle of shampoo and they have a party. And here I am with the best booze available." I've tried my best to keep Gary, from my own apartment, company.

"Why didn't everyone drink?" Karl Ove Knausgaard asked in Book Four of *My Struggle*. "Alcohol makes everything big, it is a wind blowing through your consciousness, it is crashing waves and swaying forests, and the light it transmits gilds everything you see, even the ugliest and most revolting person becomes attractive in some way, it is as if all objections and all judgments are cast aside in a wide sweep of the hand, in an act of supreme generosity, here everything, and I do mean everything, is beautiful."

Dawn Powell made a similar point in her diaries. "A person is like blank paper with secret writing," she wrote, "sometimes never brought out, other times brought out by odd chemicals."

In his novel *Submission*, Michel Houellebecq wrote, "It's hard to understand other people, to know what's hidden in their hearts, and without the assistance of alcohol it might never be done at all." Amis—a copy of his book *Everyday Drinking: The Distilled Kingsley Amis* should be in every home—put it this way: "The human race has not devised any way of dissolving barriers, getting to know the other chap fast, breaking the ice, that is one-tenth as handy and efficient as letting you and the other chap, or chaps, cease to be totally sober at about the same rate in agreeable surroundings."

America's founders understood all this. Barbara Holland, in her book *The Joy of Drinking*, reminded her readers that in 1787, the fifty-five delegates to the Constitutional Convention "adjourned to a tavern for some rest, and according to the bill they drank fifty-four bottles of Madeira, sixty bottles of claret, eight of whiskey, twenty-two of port, eight of hard cider, and seven bowls of punch so large that, it was said, ducks could swim around in them. Then they went back to work and finished founding the new Republic." Fifty-five delegates consumed fifty-four bottles of Madeira? Which founder let the side down?

\* \* \*

I've always found literary bars congenial to read about, from the Boar's Head Tavern, Falstaff's favorite in Shakespeare, down the line. The most fully realized bar in literature, to my sense of things, appears in *Jesus' Son*, Denis Johnson's brilliant and haunted book of linked short stories. It's called the Vine. It's where the narrator, adrift in a small Iowa town, finds his friends and forms alliances. It "was different every day," he comments. "Some of the most terrible things that had happened to me in my life had happened in here. But like the others I kept coming back." The best thing about the Vine was the bartender, a woman who "poured doubles like an angel, right up to the lip of a cocktail glass, no measuring." The grateful narrator says to her, "Nurse, . . . you have a lovely pitching arm." The second-best thing about the Vine was that it had no jukebox, instead "a real stereo continually playing tunes of alcoholic self-pity and sentimental divorce."

There's a fictional bar called Cervix in Shteyngart's *Super Sad True Love Story*, and one called the Cunt in Stephen King's *The Institute*. These are perhaps the American equivalent of the pubs in England named Cock and Bull. The least congenial fictional bar is depicted in *It's a Wonderful Life*, the 1946 Frank Capra movie. It was once called Martini's, but in the alternative universe in which George (James Stewart) has never been born, it's Nick's. As George enters with Clarence the Angel, the mood is grim and frantic. The bartender doesn't recognize George, who orders a double bourbon to settle his nerves. Clarence orders a flaming rum punch before he dithers and switches his order to mulled wine, "heavy on the cinnamon and light on the cloves." The bartender, who by now is annoyed, tells him, "Look, mister. We serve hard drinks in here for men who want to get drunk fast, and we don't need any characters around to give the joint atmosphere. Is that clear, or do I have to slip you my left for a convincer?" He calls George and Clarence a pair of "pixies," a code word for a different epithet.

Libraries by day, bars by night: that was the Charles Bukowski lifestyle. How do you pick a bar? Harry Crews said a good bar should never be crowded, because not enough people can recognize a good bar. The poet August Kleinzahler, a duke of dark corners, was a regular at the Zam Zam Room in San Francisco because it was known for dry martinis and for tossing people out. "It was one of the most depressing, unfriendly rooms I had ever walked into," he wrote in *Cutty, One Rock*, his memoir. "I knew immediately I had found sanctuary." A good bartender should have at least one shitty joke on tap. The bartender at the Zam Zam had this one: "What's a Dickens martini? Give up? No olive or twist."

Warren Hinckle, the muckraking editor of *Ramparts* magazine during its heyday in the late 1960s, lived in San Francisco, too, but he never mentioned the Zam Zam. Hinckle wore an eyepatch (the result of a childhood accident), kept a pet capuchin monkey named Henry Luce in the *Ramparts'* office, and sometimes worked out of a bar in North Beach called Cookie Picetti's. One observer walked into the bar with Hinckle and watched as the bartender, without prompting, set up fifteen screwdrivers, which Hinckle drank. This story strikes me as unpersuasive. Who would order like that? By the fourth or fifth drink, the rest would be lukewarm. Whenever I drink fifteen screwdrivers, I order them in batches of five, timed to arrive every twenty minutes—as I assume you do.

Frank McCourt, when he was nineteen, got thrown out of Costello's, an Irish bar on Third Avenue in Manhattan. He describes the scene in *'Tis*, his memoir, a sequel to *Angela's Ashes*. He was drinking fifteen-cent beers when the bartender mentioned Dr. Johnson. When McCourt asked who Dr. Johnson was, the bartender snatched away his glass. "Leave this bar," he said. "Walk west on Forty-second until you come to Fifth. You'll see two great stone lions. Walk up the steps between those two lions, get yourself a library card and don't be an idiot." He added: "Don't come back until you've read *The Lives of the English Poets*. Go on. Get out."

Certain staff writers at *The New Yorker*, in the mid-twentieth century, liked a gloomy nearby bar in midtown, near their offices, called the Cortile. "The Cortile was ideally suited to people with a glum view of life, and there have always been many such on the magazine," Brendan Gill wrote. The Cortile may have been the inspiration for a question *The New Yorker*'s founding editor, Harold Ross, wanted answered: "How dark is it legally permissible for a bar to be?" One dark bar I visit a lot is Fanelli's, in SoHo, the closest good bar to the Angelika Film Center, the city's best art house. In Jonathan Franzen's *The Corrections*, Fanelli's is where, at his lowest moment, Chip Lambert removes a shoplifted hunk of salmon from his pants in the men's room.

I've mentioned Jimmy's Corner, the boxing bar tucked into Times Square, in a previous chapter. The most memorable drink I've had there was alongside Salman Rushdie. This was in 2007 or 2008, almost two decades after the fatwa was proclaimed against him. He brought his editor, but no security apparatus. We sat at the bar, and the other patrons gawked. I don't remember what we talked about, but I do remember telling him that my ten-year-old son had begun to beat me at chess. Rushdie responded by saying, oracularly, that when you lose in chess, it's not just a defeat—it's a soul-defeat. Or something like that. Either way it was deflating. The second most memorable was with Anthony Bourdain, not long before he published *Kitchen Confidential* and his life blew up. He'd written a short book review for me. He wore a leather jacket and he smoked and he was undeniably handsome, but there was still an aspect of the eager Jersey kid that he was about him. He hadn't yet turned into *Anthony Bourdain*. Like me, he was a big Denis Johnson fan. Bourdain turned me on to Johnson's poetry, which I didn't know. He recommended the 1982 collection *The Incognito Lounge*. There are good drinking poems in that book, including "Heat," which includes the lines,

> *It's beautiful Susan, her hair sticky with gin,*
> *Our Lady of Wet Glass-Rings on the Album Cover.*

\* \* \*

The thing to drink at bars, most of the time, is beer. "A pint of plain is your only man," as Flann O'Brien put it. Iris Murdoch was found to be, after her death, an assiduous collector of beer mats. Patricia Highsmith liked to impress her drinking partners by tearing beer cans in two with her bare hands. Anne Sexton wrote that, most likely, "God has a brown voice, as soft and full as beer." And Eve Babitz commented, "I got deflowered on two cans of Rainier Ale." She added, "I began to wonder what else there was out there that was like Rainier Ale."

I am not a drinker of fine IPAs; they're too bitter for me, and the alcohol content is ruinously higher. "Get behind me, master brewers of Brooklyn, Portland, and Chapel Hill, you hipster hopsters," as Colson Whitehead wrote in *The Noble Hustle*, his poker book. A friend once referred to my mug of cheap beer as a Love in a Canoe, because it was "fucking close to water." Cree long ago settled on her favorite beer: Blue Moon, that crisp Belgian white, with a slice of orange. There are always two six-packs in the icebox. Myself, I fill the bottom of the fridge with colorful bottles of the industrial lagers of diverse countries.

Leave it to Toni Morrison, in *Song of Solomon*, to use beer imagery to evoke, in the earthiest terms, the end of a romance. "She was the third beer," Morrison wrote. "Not the first one, which the throat receives with almost tearful gratitude; nor the second, that confirms and extends the pleasure of the first. But the third, the one you drink because it's there, because it can't hurt, and because what difference does it make?"

A close friend was the *Times* cocktails columnist for a decade in the early aughts, the cocktail renaissance era in America, so I got to know my way around non-dive bars, too. I'd follow him all night, snaking our way through beehive Manhattan in yellow taxis, drinking on the Sulzberger family's nickel, as he worked his way around town, taste-testing well-made juleps and rickeys and cobblers and sours and fizzes and slings. It was an education. I learned, for sure, that, as Sarah M. Broom writes in *Yellow House*, "a mixed drink should be the color of the alcohol, not of the mixer." And I began to practice what might be the best bit of drinking advice I've ever heard. According to Kenneth Tynan, Humphrey Bogart would never simply hand someone a drink: he would take that person by the wrist and *screw* the drink into their hand as if it were a lamp socket. Penn, my son, is now my skilled guide through the galaxy of Manhattan's bars; he works, lucky for me, in the spirits world, and he knows all.

If your local bar now uses fresh juices and decent spirits, your restaurant has a cocktails list, and your liquor store carries sixty varieties of whiskey where it used to carry six, you have this cocktail renaissance, led by bartenders like Dale DeGroff and writers like David Wondrich, to thank. This movement has spun off some preachiness and pretension (waxed mustaches, affected tattoos, pinstripe vests, cutesy drink names, inflated bills), but it's been a small price to pay. The book that Wondrich edited, *The Oxford Companion to Spirits and Cocktails*, is one to own. Many of its entries are scholarly enough to allow you to convince yourself, and perhaps even your spouse, that your interest in getting wasted is an academic pursuit. Its editors do criticize "flair" bartending, of the sort Tom Cruise demonstrated in the 1988 movie *Cocktail*. The exception to this rule, I would stipulate, is Sam's ability, in *Cheers*, to slide a glass of beer around the corner of his bar.

* * *

When I enter a good wine store and gaze at the teeming shelves, I understand how the young, and the unread, feel when they enter a bookstore. What is all this senseless, formidable beauty? After almost four decades of purposeful wine drinking, my knowledge remains minimal. I've never had the money to buy bottles to lay down. One good decision I made, when young, was to pick an affordable French region whose wines I like—the Rhônes—and stick to them. In particular I buy any Rhône wines imported by Kermit Lynch, because (a) Kermit has a jolly and literate soul and (b) they are reliable and tend to be of good value. When I'm in doubt, I choose bottles by their labels. If a winemaker has good taste in design, it seems more likely they'll have good taste in general. This is so, eight times out of ten. I know we're belt-tightening when Cree brings home box wines, which aren't to be dismissed. Some wit on Twitter recently referred to them as "cardboardeaux."

Cree has an intelligent nose for wine. She can identify a big wine's several clear acts on her tastebuds. I like to hear her tasting notes, and I like writers who provide them. "White wine is like electricity," Joyce wrote in *Ulysses*. In *My Struggle*, Book Four, Karl Ove Knausgaard said "the taste [of white wine] was of summer nights, discos bursting at the seams, buckets of ice on the tables, gleaming eyes, tanned bare arms." A. J. Liebling described Tavel, the French rosé that was his favorite, as being "warm but dry, like an enthusiasm held under restraint." D. H. Lawrence tasted a Spanish white that he said tasted like "the sulfurous urination of some aged horse." The best tasting notes I'm aware of appear in Tony Hoagland's poem "When Dean Young Talks About Wine":

> *He says, Great first chapter but no plot.*
> *He says, Long runway, short flight.*

*He says, This one never had a secret.*
*He says, You can't wear stripes with that.*

*He squints as if recalling his childhood in France.*
*He purses his lips and shakes his head at the glass.*

Hoagland's death in 2018, at sixty-four, was a great loss to American poetry. In this poem he builds toward lines that I find almost unspeakably moving.

*But where is the Cabernet of rent checks and asthma*
    *medication?*
*Where is the Burgundy of orthopedic shoes?*
*Where is the Chablis of skinned knees and jelly*
    *sandwiches?*
*with the aftertaste of cruel Little League coaches?*
*and the undertone of rusty stationwagon?*

\* \* \*

Angela Carter was said to annoy her friends by pouring them each one glass of wine, then corking the bottle and putting it away. A character in Lorrie Moore's collection of stories *Bark* utters a line I think of every time I open a bottle: "No wine . . . It leads to cheese." Nora Ephron has written about how, during dinner parties in the 1960s and '70s, most people drank hard liquor throughout. "Nobody knew about wine," she wrote.

Wine is necessary, Virginia Woolf wrote, to "repair some of the damages of the day's living." As old age approached,

Colette was proud that she maintained "a stomach without remorse or damage, a very well-disposed liver, and a still-sensitive palate, all preserved by good and honest wine." We should all be so lucky. In her book *An Omelette and a Glass of Wine*, Elizabeth David wrote about what it was like, for a woman in the 1960s and '70s, to try to order wine without being condescended to. She recalled the waiter who asked, "A bottle, madam? A *whole* bottle? Do you know how large a whole bottle is?"

My favorite wine writer might be Auberon Waugh, son of the novelist Evelyn Waugh. The best of Auberon's work is collected in a witty book called *Waugh on Wine*. When he was the editor of a monthly magazine in London called the *Literary Review* in the 1980s, he sometimes paid his free-lance reviewers in bottles of wine, a practice I wish someone would revive. What made Waugh a great wine writer is that he told you things other wine writers didn't, such as the fact that the only wine he knew that paired brilliantly with pot was Deinhard's Hochheimer Königin Victoria Berg Riesling Kabinett.

I think I'd smoked some pot myself the night I committed the Great Wine Crime of my life. We were hosting a fortieth birthday dinner, with twenty guests, for a friend in the wine business. As a treat, she brought two bottles of an old, and rare, and dear, South African white. She opened the bottles and poured an inch into our glasses, and then, as someone rose to make a toast, I set off, from my seat next to hers, a confetti cannon. I didn't realize my grave error until the shreds of confetti, fluttering down to earth, began to fill the glasses and bleed their synthetic dyes into the wine. I still mope about my idiocy.

* * *

I prefer white goods, gin and vodka, to brown goods, but a finger of scotch or bourbon, later in the evening, is a pleasant thing. There is something uniquely American about the latter. The French writer Simone de Beauvoir made this plain in the diaries she kept while traveling in America in 1947, which she published under the title *America Day by Day*. "I don't like the taste of whiskey; I only like these glass sticks you stir it with," she wrote. "Yet until three o'clock in the morning, I drink scotch docilely because scotch is one of the keys to America. I want to break through the glass wall."

She makes the mistake of conflating scotch and bourbon. Mailer thought this a crucial error. "I'm an American writer, I drink bourbon, an American drink," he wrote. "That's the difference between a great writer and someone who'll never be a great writer: someone who knows the difference between scotch and bourbon." I suspect de Beauvoir could not have cared less. Jean-Paul Sartre, her partner in life if not marriage, made a similar comment to A. J. Liebling, who printed it in *The New Yorker*. "Two phrases only are necessary for a whole evening of English conversation, I have found: 'Scotch-and-soda?' and 'Why not?'" Sartre said. "By alternating them, it is impossible to make a mistake."

Lillian Hellman drank her scotch neat, out of a wineglass. (I know a well-known writer and academic who drinks his gin this way, albeit on ice.) Hunter S. Thompson called Chivas over shredded ice a Snow Cone. "Bourbon does for me what the piece of cake did for Proust," Walker Percy wrote. When I have a neat glass of bourbon, I recall the Emily Dickinson poem in which she requested, "Bring me the sunset in a cup."

* * *

This chapter is written, obviously, in praise of drinking. In Joseph O'Neill's excellent novel *Netherland*, the narrator comments: "We courted in the style preferred by the English: alcoholically." Muriel Spark, in *A Far Cry from Kensington*, recommended this: "It is my advice to anyone getting married," she wrote, "that they should first see the other partner when drunk."

The thinking drinker, however, knows not to take it too far. In his *Paris Review* interview, the novelist Barry Hannah, who got sober late in life, said that if he were asked to appear on television as a spokesman for anti-alcohol causes, he'd say, "Listen, if you need more than three beers, worry." Hannah makes me worry. I don't want to begin lurching around like Ray Milland in *The Lost Weekend*, my eyes like the Xs in a comic strip character's.

Dylan Thomas famously defined an alcoholic as someone you don't like who drinks as much as you do. Eve Babitz said that her friend Connie "had to fuck two midgets before she knew it was time" to join AA.

Denis Johnson is always the writer who haunts me. "If you keep drinking your babies will come out crosseyed, and you'll end up buried in a strange town with your name spelled wrong on your grave," he wrote in *The Largesse of the Sea Maiden*, his final story collection.

In the meantime, there are hangovers. In one of Robert Coover's inimitable short stories, an invisible man vomits—and this sobers everyone else up immediately. Otherwise, you're left to search Google, where you'll find a thousand home remedies, from mild palliatives (buttermilk, honey, bananas) to shock therapy (pickle juice, kudzu extract, raw cabbage). If you can drag yourself into Walgreens or Rite Aid, there's usually a potion or two that promises relief.

The problem with these cures, Kingsley Amis wrote in *On Drink*, is that they deal only with the physical manifestations of a hangover. What also urgently needs to be treated, he observed, is the metaphysical hangover—"that ineffable compound of depression, sadness (these two are not the same), anxiety, self-hatred, sense of failure and fear for the future" that looms over the grizzled morning after.

Amis's ideas for curing a physical hangover were fairly routine, though a few of the crazier ones will make you laugh. ("Go up for half an hour in an open aeroplane, needless to say with a non-hungover person at the controls.") His notions about fixing a metaphysical hangover are where things got interesting. Amis recommended, among other things, a course of "hangover reading," one that "rests on the principle that you must feel worse emotionally before you start to feel better. A good cry is the initial aim." He suggested beginning with Milton. "My own choice would tend to include the final scene of *Paradise Lost*," he wrote, "with what is probably the most poignant moment in all our literature coming at lines 624–6."

This book has investigated reading and eating and reading and drinking. I thank Amis, regularly, for his ideas about reading and recovering.

# DINNER

It is a fact of life that people give dinner parties, and when they invite you, you have to turn around and invite them back. Often they retaliate by inviting you again, and you must then extend another invitation. Back and forth you go, like Ping-Pong balls, and what you end up with is called social life.

**—LAURIE COLWIN**, *Home Cooking*

A nd so, as Samuel Pepys would say, to dinner.

Dinner was a big deal in our house, the main event, when our kids were growing up. Whole evenings were spent in the kitchen, around the center island. My daughter has written that the sound of my cocktail shaker was the dinner bell, like the summoning gong in *To the Lighthouse*. She assures me it was a jovial sound. It meant: It's time to come downstairs. It's time to sit and talk and make the cook happy. It's the evening's start. The day's mortifications and errors will be confessed and found to be relative. Judith Martin, a.k.a. Miss Manners, underscored the importance of nightly family meals. "The dinner table is the center for the teaching and practicing not just of table manners," she wrote, "but of conversation, consideration, tolerance, family feeling, and just about all the other accomplishments of polite society except the minuet."

We'll pick at cheese and crackers and nuts while the cooking progresses. If my friend Will is around, he'll remind everyone that cheese is "the fat man's candy." Thanks, Will. Cheese knives! They're dull, so you can face off with them, as Alan Bates and Roddy McDowall do in *The Collection*, the film of the Harold Pinter play. Czesław Miłosz, in his *Paris Review* interview, said that "the poet is like a mouse in an enormous cheese, excited by how much cheese there is to eat." There should be more poems like Tracy K. Smith's "In Your Condition," in which "wedge of brie" is rhymed with "Angelina Jolie." Sharp cheddar is our nightly thing, but we'll put out whatever we have. The best everyday crackers are Stoned Wheat Thins, or rather were Stoned Wheat Thins—I was disconsolate to learn (another tiny crack in civilization) that they've recently been discontinued.

Music should be playing, at least as you prepare, but beware. Gael Greene wrote about an evening with Craig Claiborne during which, while prepping dinner, he put the *West Side Story* soundtrack on his hi-fi and turned it up. When the song "Maria" (*Maria . . . Maria, Maria*) came on, Claiborne knelt at Greene's feet, acting out the lyrics with dinner theater gusto. He danced with Greene, and he danced by himself, and then he fell down a spiral staircase and ended up in the emergency room. At our house, we listened to the same playlist almost every night. It didn't get old because it contained nearly nine hundred songs, the ones I felt my kids should most know by heart, from the Staple Singers, Willie Nelson, and Emmylou Harris to Prince, the White Stripes, and the Mekons, and so on for hours. I considered it a part of their education, a fun part, and I'm glad I did. I still update this playlist, which I've dubbed "Canonicity" on Sonos. It's a rough draft of the songs I'd like to have played at my funeral service. I rarely played Bruce Springsteen for my kids at home, because I like him too much, and I didn't want to be *that guy*. (I told them to go and find Springsteen on their own.) While cranking "Sherry

Darling" I might have ecstatically tripped, like Claiborne, down the staircase and into our basement.

*  *  *

How should one be in the kitchen? "A suave performer never looks hurried," Julia Child wrote. I rarely feel suave. "Stand tall and make small, deliberate movements," Bill Buford was told in Lyon. "Be easy in your body when you cook." I am rarely easy in my body. Nigella Lawson remarked that this sort of ease requires practice. "Too many people cook only when they're giving a dinner party," she wrote. "And it's very hard to go from zero to a hundred miles an hour. How can you learn to feel at ease around food, relaxed about cooking, if every time you go into the kitchen it's to cook at competition level?" She's right. Even over the course of writing this book I've grown calmer at the stove (I've also gained ten pounds) because I've been inspired to cook so much.

The Maine writer John Thorne is among my culinary heroes. The recipes in his books, which include *Outlaw Cook* and *Serious Pig*, take the form of gentle, offbeat personal essays. He takes humble foods and scrutinizes them until they begin to glow. In his book *Simple Cooking*, Thorne says we should always cook as if we were being observed, in the same way we were "brought up to wear clean underpants in case we got hit by a bus." Someone might show up. I've spent a lot of time in my kitchen life, when alone, imagining someone might show up, the way a kid alone on a basketball court becomes an announcer manqué (*Two seconds left . . . he's trapped in the corner*). I imagine blowing my just-popping-in friends away with the classic French bouillabaisse I happened to have simmering on the stove, or with something miraculous I've pulled from the oven. "Here's one I made earlier," as the television chefs like to say. I like to imagine I'm cooking as well as does Louise, a character in Fran Ross's novel *Oreo*. Her cooking *destroys* people. "Five people in the neighborhood went insane from the bouquets that wafted to them from Louise's kitchen," Ross writes. "Three men and a woman had to be chained up by their families." Later, on a train, another man tastes Louise's food—her "Apollonian stuffed grape leaves, her revolutionary piroshki"—and says: "Oh my God, it's so good I'm coming in my pants."

The novelist Bob Shacochis, in *Domesticity: A Gastronomic Interpretation of Love*, a collection of the come-as-you-are food columns he wrote for *Esquire* in the 1980s and '90s, said that he didn't like others in the kitchen while he cooked. "My sense of the culinary environment mirrors a pilot's notion of a cockpit," he wrote. "If you have no good reason to be in there, or don't know what you're doing, better get lost fast." I'm more in league with Alexandre Dumas. When Dumas was cooking, he was known to race around and crack jokes and enlist everyone as a potential sous-chef. The more the merrier. (Stanley Kubrick was the same way.) Sometimes Dumas would vanish for thirty minutes. He'd be found at his writing table, finishing a chapter. Christopher Hitchens was known to get up from his *own dinner party* and dash off a column. These took him about forty-five minutes. I edited Hitchens a half dozen times when I worked for the *Times Book Review*. I suspect he wrote his reviews for me in less time than that. Those pieces were nonetheless pointed, funny, full of life, and better than almost everyone else's. Life isn't fair that way.

*   *   *

Julia Child's husband, Paul, would read to her while she was cooking. In a 1953 letter, she wrote that they were about to finish *Boswell in Holland*, excerpts from the journals James Boswell kept while living in that country in 1763 and 1764. I've since read *Boswell in Holland*. There's not much food in it, but there's a lot about cultivating the so-called manly virtues—reticence, calm, a certain seriousness—in case one needs bucking up. *Boswell in Holland* reads like the once-popular dating book *The Rules*, except for ambitious young men. Some nights we read aloud in our kitchen, a short story or something menu-appropriate. On a snowy night not long ago, I talked Hattie into making taquitos—those rolled-up, deep-fried, crunchy little snackerels. (Half my waking hours are spent cajoling other people into cooking things for me, hinting, begging, pleading, bargaining.) Taquitos are a process. While Hattie worked, to keep her company, I sat on a stool and read aloud Eve Babitz's paean to her favorite L.A. taquito joint. It's long and you can find it in *Eve's Hollywood*. I'll just remark that it contains the line, "You could be blind and deaf and that still leaves you the taquitos."

By evening, at our house, there are usually cookbooks open all over the place. Sylvia Plath was said to strew open cookbooks around this way. "A really good cookbook," Jan Morris wrote in *Pleasures from a Tangled Life*, "is intellectually more adventurous than the *Kama Sutra*." We own so many, yet I use the same eight or nine, with the occasional recipe plucked from a stray website thrown in. I'm increasingly determined to use cookbooks and not rely on the web for anonymous recipes and all the ads and extended prologues that attend them. There's a website called Eat Your Books that helps. You tell it the cookbooks you own and then, when you're looking for a recipe or a use for an ingredient, you type it into the Eat Your Books search engine and, presto, it searches through your own books for recipes. It's like having a sous-chef solely devoted to research. More and more I try to leave recipes behind, as Cree has—she considers them insults to her instincts. Still, I cling to Julian Barnes's definition of cooking, in his book *The Pedant in the Kitchen*, as "the transformation of uncertainty (the recipe) into certainty (the dish) via fuss." I like certainty, and I don't mind fuss.

\* \* \*

For every good cook in literature, there's a dismal one. The pages fill with what Stanley Elkin, in his novel *The Dick Gibson Show*, called "a vagrant smell of the amiss." "She did not try to make her meals nauseating; she simply didn't know how not to," Toni Morrison writes in *Song of Solomon*. In *A Confederacy of Dunces*, Ignatius J. Reilly complains, "Mother doesn't cook . . . She burns." In *Breakfast at Tiffany's*, the meals Holly Golightly serves include a "tobacco tapioca." The book's unnamed narrator, a writer who loves her, comments: "best not to describe it." A bad meal can scorch the spirit. "The humor I am in is worse than words can describe," Charlotte Brontë wrote in an 1841 letter. "I have had a hideous dinner of some abominable, spiced-up mess, and it has exasperated me against the world at large." In his biography of James Merrill, Langdon Hammer writes that the poet "reprised leftovers with the stinginess of a rich Yankee—improvised concoctions that sometimes seemed like pranks. In the kitchen, as at his desk, he was averse to throwing things away. More than once, when a casserole crashed on the way to the table, he picked out the shards of glass or crockery, and served it to his guests with a smile." In one of Thomas McGuane's short stories, a character says, "That food was so bad I can't wait for it to become a turd and leave me."

Ruth Reichl's memoir *Tender at the Bone* is about being raised by a mother known behind her back as "the Queen of Mold," famous for sickening her guests. There is something triumphant about a terrible meal, Laurie Colwin wrote. About a bad dinner in Lyon, Buford wrote in *Dirt*, he stood up and congratulated the staff and a chef who had wandered out "for having produced one of the rudest, ugliest, most unpleasant meal experiences that I could remember having suffered in a long time. 'Congratulations!' I said." He grabbed the maître d's head between his hands and "kissed him robustly on both cheeks."

The worst meal of my life—the one I most regret, at any rate—I consumed in November 2016, election night. Michel Houellebecq's narrator, in his novel *Submission*, says, "I've always loved election night. I'd go so far to say it's my favorite TV show, after the World Cup finals." I'm in total agreement. I was so certain Hillary Clinton would triumph over the Cheez Whiz Caligula that I shopped for a celebratory meal for one. (Cree wanted to make her own election-night dinner.) At no small expense I gathered the makings of a chilled seafood platter: oysters, littlenecks, large shrimp, a lobster that I cooked, cooled, and split, a couple of blue crab claws. I began to eat the whole production on ice with a bottle of better-than-usual white wine while the results trickled in. My stomach churned as it became clear that the unthinkable was thinkable. I tried different channels, hoping the news would be better elsewhere in the multiverse. It wasn't. The West Virginian in me became disgusted at my own presumption, at my lobster-fork liberalism. I ate penitential lentils for days afterward.

*   *   *

There was a long stretch, during and after Covid, when people stopped having full-on dinner parties. I wasn't certain I missed them. For too many years we threw the sort of dinner parties that demolish a weekend—the kind you spend all of Saturday preparing for and all of Sunday recovering from, physically, financially, and emotionally, after you've politely shooed the last guest, in the morning, off the downstairs couch. Covid has brought out misanthropic tendencies, in myself and others I know. I'm more in sync than I used to be with dinner-party despisers. William Golding, the author of *Lord of the Flies*, was among these. Golding was uncomfortable socially—he wanted to bomb the cocky princelings at Eton, his old school, he wrote, with "a mile or two of wire, a few hundred tons of TNT, and one of those plunger-detonating machines which makes the user feel like Jehovah"—and he disliked public occasions. When he did go out, Golding could behave memorably. After a 1971 dinner party, he destroyed a puppet of Bob Dylan that belonged to his host. "He had woken in the middle of the night," his biographer wrote, "attacked it under the impression that it was Satan, and buried it in the back garden." John Updike disliked dinner parties, too, or at least what he called "those late dinner parties (we sat down at ten) with which the Manhattan rich prove their fortitude."* Unlike Updike, I like eating this late. In summertime there's time to wander around outside, enjoying the fading evening and perhaps finding the hidden pistol in your host's shed. Angela Carter wrote that she loved to see her guests "walking round the garden with glasses in their hands" because it "fulfills some deep bourgeois fantasy of mine."

The case against dinner parties is best argued by Phillip Lopate, in his essay "Against Joie de Vivre." His parents didn't throw dinner parties when he was growing up. (Mine didn't, either.) Maybe that's why, he writes, he finds them smug, boring, decadent, awkward, and hypocritical. "The smugness begins as soon as one enters the door, since one is already part of the chosen few," he wrote. "And from then on, every mechanical step in dinner-party process is designed to augment the atmosphere of group amour-propre." *Oh no*, he thinks to himself, we're going to talk about the latest *New Yorker* in-depth piece. He skewers this sort of evening: "People who ordinarily would not spare a moment worrying about the

---

* The hour you eat sends class signals. The definitively middle-class Portnoy family in Philip Roth's novel dined exactly at six. So does where you eat. In *Matilda*, Roald Dahl stigmatizes her parents by having them eat frozen dinners in front of the television set.

treatment of schizophrenics in mental hospitals, the fate of Great Britain in the Common Market, or the disposal of nuclear wastes suddenly find their consciences orchestrated in unison about these problems, thanks to their favorite periodical—though a month later they have forgotten all about it and are on to something new."

* * *

Lopate was eating with the wrong people. M. F. K. Fisher argued, in *Serve It Forth*, that dinner companions should be "chosen for their ability to eat—and drink!" They should also "possess the rare gift of sitting." Four hours at the table should be nothing to them. If your friends are squeamish eaters, Colwin said, "change friends instantly and find some red-blooded chowhounds with few scruples and no interest in health." As often as possible, you want to have your closest friends over; everybody eats more when no strangers are at the table. Bernardo Bertolucci, the Italian film director, said about his friends, "My university is having dinner every night with Elsa Morante, Alberto Moravia and Pier Paolo Pasolini." And yet, there's some truth to Eugene Walter's comment, in *Milking the Moon*, that "if everybody knows everybody at a party, then it's not a party. It's only a family reunion."

What you want are people as good at talking as eating. Tina Brown, in *The Vanity Fair Diaries*, wrote, "I want one Falstaff for every Hal, one pauper for every billionaire, one young Turk for every legendary old sacred cow." Not everyone can attract the kinds of A-list guests Brown can. At least once a year, before Covid, that is, I would cold-call, or rather cold-email, someone I've admired but don't know, and ask him or her to dinner. Usually, they said yes. The *Times Book Review* likes to ask people what writers, past or present, they'd invite to a dinner party. Mine would lean toward the brilliant and jolly—Dr. Johnson, Molly Ivins, A. J. Liebling, Colette, Albert Murray, Jim Harrison, Christopher Hitchens—the ones who'd linger for hours at the table. Ideally we'd all be smoking.

Auden, in his poem "Tonight at Seven-Thirty," has advice about inviting people. A god, for example, would be a bad guest because

> *he would be too odd*
> *to talk to and, despite his imposing presence, a bore.*

What you want at the table, Auden continued, is at least one raconteur "in a talkative mood but knowing when to stop," a world-traveler to "interject now and then / a sardonic comment" and most importantly

> *. . . men*
> *and women who enjoy the cloop of corks, appreciate*
> *dapatical\* fare, yet can see in swallowing*
> *a sign act of reverence.*

There are people you don't want at your table. Clarice Lispector was said to be a pretentious dinner guest. She would show up late and leave almost immediately. According to her biographer, one host made a borscht in her honor, a salute

---

\* "Dapatical," according to the *OED*, is obsolete but means "sumptuous."

to her "Slavic origins." She took a bite, pronounced it delicious, then didn't touch it. After she left, her host said, "I felt I had survived once again." To sit next to V. S. Naipaul was dangerous; his wit could shred. In case you're insulted at the table, practice the look Noël Coward used while delivering a reply; it was said to resemble "a dead albatross." John Guare recalled a dinner during which Naipaul tried to stump the other guests by posing three literary questions: 1. What is the only food mentioned in *Wuthering Heights*? 2. What is the occupation of Madame Bovary's daughter? 3. How does Swann dispense with his mistress?* The first two questions were met with silence. When the third was asked, the director Louis Malle recited a passage of *Swann's Way*. Naipaul bowed and said, "At least someone knows an answer." Years later, Guare and Naipaul met at another dinner and Guare greeted him by asking, "What is the only food mentioned in *Wuthering Heights*?"

The dread event at a table is silence. In *Mating*, Norman Rush described "the freezing horror that seizes us when the conversation during a date or at a dinner party falters." Worse is when everyone else is talking and you are uniquely stranded. Tom Wolfe described this situation in *The Bonfire of the Vanities*. I've been there, and this hurts to read:

> He was facing social death once more. He was a man sitting utterly solo at a dinner table. The hive buzzed all around him. Everyone else was in a state of social bliss. Only he was stranded. Only he was a wallflower

---

* 1. Gruel. 2. She works in a factory. 3. He tells her she is not his type.

with no conversational mate, a social light of no watt-age whatsoever . . . *My life is coming apart!* . . . The shame!

The Washington hostess Sally Quinn, in her book *The Party*, calls the seat between two bores the "gristle" seat, words that are hard to forget once you've read them. What to do if you're stuck in a gristle seat? The writer and editor Virginia Faulkner had this advice: "I ask the gentleman on my right, Are you a bed-wetter? And when we have exhausted that topic, I remark to the gentleman on my left, You know, I spit blood this morning." The diplomat Jerry Wadsworth once asked, as a final conversational gambit, "Do you like string?" *National Review* ran a competition for the remark or question most likely to warm up talk with a dinner companion. The winner was, "If you had your life to live over again, would you have come tonight?" A runner-up was, "Is ground glass shiny after being cooked?" Bores are a bummer. Worse are the solipsists who spend two hours over lunch and never ask a question, leaving you to simply try to interview them.

\* \* \*

Nearly every book about entertaining says, correctly enough, that the best tables are for six to eight people, small enough for general conversation. Nora Ephron understood why. "If you have people to dinner and make good food and then put your guests at a long rectangular table where people at one end can't hear what's going on at the other end and are pretty much trapped talking to the person on either side of themselves—well, what is the point?" she wrote. "But put them at a round table, and at some point in the evening you can have one conversation. With any luck at all, the funniest person in the room will tell a great story and everyone will fall on the floor laughing and go home believing they've gone to one of the best dinners of their lives."

We have a round wooden table that seats eight and, with leaves, fourteen, if everyone keeps in their elbows. It is in slight disrepair; one side droops, just noticeably. Otherwise, it resembles the one around which Charlie Rose did his nightly interviews on PBS. After Charlie's fall from grace ("I'm from the South, we're touchers"), the jokes about that stopped. On her tables Cree likes small individual flowers and cuttings from plants, and has a collection of vases for them. Ann Beattie has said she likes to scatter her tables, at dinners, with figurines: miniature people, animals, and houses. "I like those tiny stamped and die-cut sitting figures," she said. "I place them in a long row, for a crazy centerpiece, and by the end of the dinner everyone has arranged them in little groups. When I clear the table, I invariably find all the little people copulating."

\* \* \*

When I'm traveling, or Cree is away, I live for eating alone, though many find the experience painful. Pepys's diaries are filled with laments such as, "Dined alone; sad for want of company and not being very well, and know not how to eat alone," and, "When I come to be alone, I do not eat in time, nor enough, nor with any good heart, and I immediately begin to be full of wind." In Barbara Pym's *Excellent Women*, a character receives bad news about a romance and dines alone on cod, because "cod seemed a suitable dish for a rejected one and I ate it humbly." Alone, I can cook something Cree would go out of her way to avoid. I'll make Betty Fussell's hamburger au poivre or the poet Ricardo Sanchez's pungent *chili con verde* or a pot of Harrison's Caribbean stew, which is essentially a pailful of ribs and sausages and chicken swimming in buttery hot sauce, and it spawns leftovers for days. It's nice to cook without feeling Alice Waters is peeking over your shoulder.

Katherine Mansfield, in a journal entry from 1919, described this kind of freedom. "This joy of being alone," she wrote. "What is it? I feel so gay and at peace—the whole house takes the air. Lunch is ready. I have a baked egg, apricots and cream, cheese straws and black coffee. How delicious! A baby meal!" When alone, I'm not like Henry Markowitz, the shop manager in Allegra Goodman's story collection *The Family Markowitz*, who sets the table for himself and lights candles. That would make me feel ridiculous. I do, however, fold a napkin. Better to eat at a restaurant's bar when you're solo, especially if the restaurant is thrumming and alive. I like being a party of one. It's a chance to be solitary and steeped in humanity at the same time. It's a chance to observe the ballet of dinner service—which, as Kazuo Ishiguro notes in *The Remains of the Day*, runs along "that balance between attentiveness and the illusion of absence." I'll have the bar nuts, a martini, some clams, the ricotta cavatelli. I used to order the shepherd's pie until I read Bourdain. "Shepherd's pie?" he wrote. "Sounds like leftovers to me."

I'll make sure to have something to read that isn't my phone. It's rare to see a person with a book or magazine these days;

it's like glimpsing a wolf in the forest. Yasmina Reza, in her play *God of Carnage*, has a character complain that "men are so wedded to their gadgets . . . It belittles them . . . It takes away all their authority . . . A man ought to give the impression he's alone." If you're alone at a table and can spread out, a newspaper will do. The feed salesman in Philip Larkin's poem "Livings" orders

> *One beer, and then "the dinner," at which I read*
> *The —shire Times from soup to stewed pears.*
> *Births, deaths. For sale. Police court. Motor spares.*

Reading a broadsheet paper at a bar, unless you've mastered the origami-art of folding it into quadrants, as people used to do on the subways, is close to impossible. I wish all restaurants were like the one in Savannah where I ate in the midnineties. Seeing that I was alone, the headwaiter brought over a tray of magazines to select from. He didn't have *Creem*, but he did have *The New Yorker*, *Newsweek*, and *The Atlantic*. When the food writer James Villas went undercover as a waiter in 1972 for *Town & Country* magazine, he discovered that "singles are never loved, contrary to what anybody says." Once you've been seated at a table, Bruce Jay Friedman wrote, "there will follow The Single Most Heartbreaking Moment in Dining Out Alone—when the second setting is whisked away and yours is spread out a bit to make the table look busier." When Friedman had to eat alone, he wrote, he'd pretend to be a restaurant critic. "The ideal table will allow you to keep your back to the wall so that you can see if anyone is laughing at you."

Sometimes I'll read a novel over dinner. Walter Benjamin opposed this practice. "One may, if necessary, read the newspaper while eating," he wrote. "But never a novel. These are two conflicting obligations." In a Nashville restaurant I once sat near a young woman reading a Barry Hannah novel at the bar. I reported this to Cree, who told me she was hit on mercilessly, when younger, when she tried to read a novel in a restaurant or bar. M. F. K. reported similar experiences. She loved reading in restaurants, "everything from *Tropic of Cancer* to *Riders of the Purple Sage*," but found that lecherous men and sometimes women "sniffed at the high wall of my isolation," forcing her to flee. Fisher was proud of her wiles as a solo diner. She was assertive; she ordered food that some considered "masculine," as well as "good wines, or good drinkin'-likka, and beers and ales." She reported that "all these reasons, and probably a thousand others, like the way I wear my hair and what shade my lipstick is, make people look strangely at me, resentfully, with a kind of hurt bafflement, when I dine alone."

My favorite thing to read, alone in a restaurant, is a restaurant review.

I wish I'd been living in Los Angeles when Jonathan Gold was writing restaurant criticism for the *Los Angeles Times*. You can catch up with his stuff in *Counter Intelligence: Where to Eat in the Real Los Angeles*. You'll understand why he was the first food critic to win the Pulitzer Prize in criticism. God, he was funny. He described the patrons in one bad and expensive restaurant as "a vivid cross-section of people who wouldn't have talked to you in high school." I also wish I'd been living in London when Kingsley Amis was writing restaurant criticism. A few of his columns from the 1980s are collected in *The Amis Collection*. They're still worth reading. "It is tempting to say that a good restaurant, like a good novel or a good poem, is recognizable straight away, as soon as you cross the threshold," Amis wrote. In another review, he described a supercilious waiter.

> He imparted an international flavor, being very much the Frenchman in his obvious surprise, even disapproval, on hearing what I proposed to eat. British in bringing the wrong things and in not apologizing when this was pointed out, and French again in implying that differences at such a low level were pretty unimportant.

After quoting a food writer saying, "A Hong Kong meal . . . is a statement to which customers are secondary," Amis writes: "I know that sort of meal, and the statement is Fuck You, and you don't have to go to Hong Kong for it. Soho is far enough."

I once asked the critic Clive James, while lunching with him at his home in Cambridge (he served little shrimps on toast), to name his favorite restaurant critics. He couldn't think of one. He looked down on the form, he said. He didn't think there was enough in food, intellectually or emotionally, to sustain a career. Anthony Bourdain said something similar: "Writing incessantly about food is like writing porn. How many adjectives can there be before you repeat yourself?" I mentioned Clive James's comments to Greil Marcus, the music critic. Marcus has never, to the best of my knowledge, written about food, although he has served on the board of directors at Chez Panisse. He disagreed and in reply sent me a xeroxed packet of the work of Dara Moskowitz Grumdahl, a Minneapolis food critic and a favorite of his. I've lost that packet, but I recall Moskowitz describing one dish as "a personal reinvention of the world that fits into the square inch at the end of a fork." With that she had me in the palm of her hand. Raymond Sokolov, a *Times* restaurant critic in the 1970s, felt the sting of the cultural prejudice against food criticism, keener then than now. In *Steal the Menu: A Memoir of Forty Years in Food*, he complained that until he became a food critic he'd been viewed as a serious person, an intellectual, someone who'd been to Harvard and Oxford. He remembers Pauline Kael coming up to him and asking, "Since when did you become a food queen?"

If I can't read new food criticism, hand me a food critic's memoir. The friskiest is Gael Greene's *Insatiable*, about being a food critic for *New York* magazine in the 1970s and '80s. Greene had sex with Elvis Presley, Burt Reynolds, and Clint Eastwood. She sometimes slept with chefs whose restaurants she was reviewing. She was open about this. One of her reviews was titled, "I Love Le Cirque, But Can I Be Trusted?" A friend once told her he had seen graffiti in a restaurant's men's room that read, "Gael Greene uses a thesaurus." Another *New York* magazine critic, Adam Platt, wrote a good memoir. His is titled *The Book of Eating: Adventures in Professional Gluttony*. Platt is excellent on the downsides of restaurant reviewing. He mentions the time a fellow eater accidentally spit gristle into his eye, giving him blurry vision for two weeks.

I'm a regular at the bars of certain restaurants. I was devastated to read, in Bill Buford's *Heat*, that when the expediter shouts "Bar loser, tender," it means that the solo guy has ordered the pork tenderloin. So often the literature of dining out alone is the literature of heartbreak. In his novel *Serotonin*, Michel Houellebecq wrote that "having a seafood platter on your own is scraping the barrel—even Françoise Sagan couldn't have described that, it's too dreadful for words." In Billy Collins's "The Fish," an elderly waiter brings a man's meal to his table; it stares up "with its one flat, iridescent eye."

> *I feel sorry for you, it seemed to say,*
> *eating alone in this awful restaurant*
> *bathed in such unkindly light*
> *and surrounded by these dreadful murals of Sicily.*

\* \* \*

In the last chapter I wrote about Gary Shteyngart's sense that the great literary drinkers are fading from view. I have a similar sense that the great gastronomes have passed away; where once were dinosaurs, there are geckos. I sometimes like to think I'm communing, when dining alone, with the kind of people Francine Prose has called "the superheroes of gluttony." Milton was among them; he likened ravenousness to wisdom. "Big eaters win," Maxine Hong Kingston wrote in *The Woman Warrior*. She mentions "Chou Yi-han of Changchow, who fried a ghost." Once I ate a meal with Cree and her father at the sorely missed Manhattan restaurant Fleur de Sel that was so perfectly tasty that, after a short pause to marshal our resources, we ordered the whole thing over again, dessert and all. For once I felt in league with Liebling.

Among writers, Thackeray was perhaps the most committed glutton, a kind of sybaritic emperor. He compared novels to sweets, and "all people with healthy literary appetites love them." His first published short story, "The Professor," was about a man who could never get enough shellfish. Thackeray proposed, in *Punch*, only half-jokingly, that Cambridge University should establish a chair dedicated to inquiry into eating. He loved people—statesmen, poets, historians, judges—"who are great at the dinner-table as in the field." There's something steadying about a strong eater. Muriel Spark described a woman who "ate steadily on as one who proves, by eating on during another's distress, the unshakable sanity of their advice." Mario Puzo was a legendary trencherman. If friends were late to meet him for dinner at a Chinese restaurant, he'd slip around the corner for a quick pizza. After he became wealthy, he had his own mozzarella man, because fresh (unrefrigerated) mozzarella is hard to find. "After fifteen minutes," he correctly told his friend Bruce Jay Friedman, "it starts to lose its freshness." As a host, Friedman wrote, Puzo "would order every pasta on the restaurant menu, so that his guests would be able to sample each one." The food scenes in *The Godfather* were mesmerizing and influenced those in *The Sopranos*. In Patricia Lockwood's novel *No One Is Talking About This*, the narrator watches five episodes of *The Sopranos* on HBO and "immediately wanted to be involved in organized crime. Not the shooting part, the part where they all sat around in restaurants."

"I'm very fond of my food," Auden said in his *Paris Review* interview. "Poets sure do throw down around the table," Kevin Young wrote, in part because they don't know where their next meal will come from. Henry, the semi-autobiographical hero of the poems in John Berryman's *The Dream Songs*, is such a thrower-down. "I write with my stomach," he declares. He loves good bread with olive oil and sliced onion. We read that he "bolted lunch, & pigged dinner" and had "meat at midnight," alongside "avocado lemon'd, artichoke hearts, / anything inner." Society appreciates a jovial male eater and makes room for him. It is, alas, usually somewhat wary of jovial female eaters. In one of Jean Stafford's short stories, a large woman envies the restraint of her slim friend. The woman thinks, "Did she know the terror and the remorse that followed on the heels of it when one slyly sneaked the lion's share of buttered toast at tea? Had she ever desired the whole of a pudding meant for twelve and hated with all her heart the others at the dinner table?" She is nearly suicidal at the fact that she is, in her words, the "wretched butterball." She should have been emulating Colette, who proudly declared, "*Je suis gourmette, gourmande, gloutonne.*"

\* \* \*

The rock critic Robert Christgau, in his memoir, *Going into the City*, talked about how he liked high literary styles by writing, "I preferred my prose with extra wontons." The poet Thom Gunn spoke of simpler prose when he referred to one of his poems as written "in my Elizabethan dumpling manner—compressed and plain." All of which is to say that, when I'm in New York, I always wish I were in Chinatown with a book of poems in my pocket.

One of the most moving scenes in Ha Jin's novel *Waiting*, which won a National Book Award in 1999, takes place in a restaurant. *Waiting* is a love story set in Communist China during the Cultural Revolution. Lin, an army doctor, falls in love with Manna, a nurse, during a forced march. They long to marry, but Lin has a wife back home—an illiterate, foot-bound peasant he was forced to wed young in an arranged marriage. Every year, for eighteen years, Lin returns home seeking a divorce, and every year he is denied. Adultery is a crime; Lin and Manna can only pine for each other. One day they decide to meet for a meal ("They would have a few cold dishes—pork head, pickled mushrooms, baby eggplants, and salted duck eggs. As for the entrée they ordered dumplings stuffed with pork, dried shrimps, cabbage, and scallions") and find themselves staring in amazement at each other. Lin looks at Manna and "realized she was thinking the same thought—this was the first time they had eaten together in a restaurant." Sometimes in Chinatown I imagine I see another Lin and Manna. I was lucky to be sent to Atlanta, where he lived, to interview Jin not long after *Waiting* came out. He told me that when he arrived in America from China, he knew America was an affluent nation because squirrels were frolicking everywhere and no one was eating them.

The chef Eddie Huang, in his memoir *Fresh Off the Boat*, makes a crucial point about certain Chinese dishes. After he consumes a Taiwanese Dan-Dan soup, with clear pork-bone stock, sesame paste, crushed peanuts, pickled radish, and scallions, he notes that it's transcendent not because the chef "used the best produce or protein or because it was locally sourced, but because he worked his dish." Sometimes a dish is a matter of playing the cards you hold well. You've got to put the whole crooked timber of your humanity into it. Huang delivers this put-down to the Alice Waters school of luminous shopping: "You can't buy a championship." For those of us who try to cook authentic Chinese food at home, Gish Jen has warned not to attempt making wonton skins yourself "unless you lack frustration in your life."

Black men and women, in midcentury New York City, often ate in Chinese and Japanese restaurants because they felt welcome there. Simone de Beauvoir has described spending an evening in Manhattan in 1947 with her friend the novelist Richard Wright. "He comes to fetch me at the hotel, and I observe that in the lobby he attracts untoward notice," she wrote. "If he asked for a room here, he would surely be refused." They eat in a Chinese restaurant because they fear they would not be served elsewhere. When Odetta was recording her album *It's a Mighty World* at RCA studios on Twenty-Fourth Street, she and her band would head every night, in the wee hours, to an all-night Japanese restaurant near Times Square. Her producer, Jack Somer, recalled that they always ordered the same thing. "It was steamed sea bass and everybody would pluck the fish off the body with chopsticks." He recalls that the bassist Raphael "Les" Grinage would ceremoniously pluck out the eyes and eat them. "He was from somewhere in the South where it was normal and everyday procedure," Somer remembered. "Sometimes it rather spoiled my appetite, but after you've been recording all night, you get hungry."

* * *

One of the great literary correspondences is between Ralph Ellison and his friend the critic Albert Murray. Their ardent letters are collected in a book called *Trading Twelves*. Food, like jazz, prose, and the blues, was never far from their thoughts. From Rome, Ellison wrote to Murray that he longed for "a belly full of that righteous cuisine—con cornbread, con buttermilk, con mustard greens." Food, for them, was a lingua franca, and a source of instant nostalgia. In his book *South to a Very Old Place*, Murray recalls from his youth the "barbecue pits and beer-seasoned chicken-shack tables; with skillets of sizzling mullets or bream or golden crisp oysters plus grits and butter; and with such white potato salads and such sweet potato pies as only downhome folks remember from picnics and association time camp meetings." Edna Lewis, in *The Taste of Country Cooking*, underlines Murray's point. "Over the years since I left home . . . , I have kept thinking about the people I grew up with and about our way of life," she wrote. "I realize how much the bond that held us had to do with food."

Rita Dove, in her poem "Family Reunion," latches onto that nostalgia, recalling

> it's understood "potluck" means
> resurrecting the food
> we've abandoned along the way
> for the sake of sleeker thighs.

The African American foundations of so much of what everyone cooks and eats in America have, at last, begun to rise toward the surface. Jessica B. Harris, in *High on the Hog*, traces how so many of our staple foods, from rice and yams to cereals, came here with slaves. We are slowly moving past what she terms "culinary apartheid." In her book *The Jemima Code*, Toni Tipton-Martin collects and peruses hundreds of early cookbooks by Black authors. Martin dispels the stereotype of the illiterate "Aunt Jemima" who cooked by instinct. Black cooks had intent and expertise. The best of their recipes were stolen—they simply disappeared, uncredited, into white cookbooks for white audiences. Another crucial book is *The Cooking Gene*, by Michael W. Twitty. Twitty is as obsessive about early African American food as Robert Caro is about LBJ. He searches long and hard for early influences. Influences are harder to confront for Black cooks, he writes, because "going to your source is traumatic."

Twitty is great on food and music. About being in the kitchen during his childhood, he wrote, "Hugh Masekela and Miriam Makeba joined Lena Horne and Kraftwerk and Afrika Bambaataa and Devo on the record player below the African paintings. Depending on who cooked in the kitchen, the tenor of the music changed. I heard gut-bucket blues and classical music and I could identify Isaac Hayes (*Hot Buttered Soul*), Carole King (*Tapestry*), and Al Green (*I'm Still in Love with You*) from album covers. Come on the right day and you could hear Billy Joel and Chic." In her introduction to *Vibration Cooking*, Vertamae Smart-Grosvenor gives "special thanks to richie havens, wilson pickett, johnny ace, la lupe, john coltrane and miss billie holiday for singing and playing everyday as i sat in my corner in the kitchen trying to get my thing together." I've written that we made a point to fill our kitchen up every night with the best music we knew. Kids are your last captive audience. My kids have their own taste now, in a big way, but enough of ours has stuck that we have a common language about it all. They often go to the houses of friends and report back that no music was playing. It felt strange to them, as if the house were dead.

Music in restaurants is a vexed topic. If it's well chosen and the acoustics are good and it doesn't blot out conversation, it's nice. Even death metal works if you can talk over it. Jonathan Gold paid attention to restaurant music like no one else. He was the Virgil Thomson of Los Angeles's Pico Boulevard. In the kind of vernacular restaurants he loved, the sound of corny music—Air Supply, let's say—generally meant the food would be terrific. He commented that "bad reggae may be the universal language." He always took note of the speakers in fake rocks. One restaurant Gold admired played "the kind of music you'd imagine lava lamps would probably make if you found a way to run them through your stereo." At another place, the thumping sounded like "Led Zeppelin played backward and underwater." He makes you want those records.

I walked out of a chic downtown Manhattan restaurant not long ago, with friends, before we'd ordered, because the music was so loud we were reduced to making hand signals. Four gestures I remember making (the extent of my sign language) were: "thumbs down," "knife across throat," "this is bullshit," and "let's get out of here." The cacophony, increasingly, is the point. It's a way to keep out the oldies, of which now, I suppose, we were. When I'm trapped in a restaurant that's playing shitty songs at defenestrating volume, I think longingly of the house rules at St. John, Fergus Henderson's restaurant in London: "No art. No music." To crib a line from the poet William Matthews, the jukebox plays Marcel Marceau.

* * *

The ending of a book, the professor Andrew Lytle told Harry Crews, "should fall off the tree like a ripe pear." Let's move toward the exits by talking about food and sex, to get a bit of some last steam under the lid of the pot, and food and death. It's very hard to read during sex unless your lover is tattooed. The problem with death, as I've mentioned earlier, is that you can't take a book with you.

Writers often reach for food imagery when trying to describe the pheromonal, lip-smacking sensations of sex. "Peeling the layers of an onion, spooning out the marrow of a beef bone, laying bare the skeleton of a salmon were acts very like the act of sex," Betty Fussell wrote in *My Kitchen Wars*, her memoir, "ecstatically fusing body and mind." I like it, too, when writers serve up images that evoke sexual disgust. Sylvia Plath's heroine, in *The Bell Jar*, makes eye contact with her first penis and it does not live up to expectations: "The only thing I could think of was turkey neck and turkey gizzards and I felt very depressed." Tom Wolfe was on a similar wavelength. He liked to employ the word "giblets" in his sex descriptions, as if it were perpetually Thanksgiving. In *Hooking Up*, Wolfe wrote, a porn magazine is crammed with "stiffened giblets" and "glistening nodes." Robert Christgau used similar imagery in a terrific description of making out with the woman he would marry. He called it "a polymorphous game of button-button with sweetmeats at the end." In Jane Smiley's novel *Ten Days in the Hills*, a penis is more prepossessing: "It lay over to the side," she writes, "not a straight, evenly shaped sausage, but more of a baguette, bulging comfortably in the middle and then narrowing just below the cap."*

In one of her poems,† Rita Dove, talking about vaginas, refers to "my prodigious scallops." In her novel *Pond*, Claire-Louise Bennett wrote that oranges are what you want to eat after a lot of sex, because "they cut through the fug and smell very organized." I can remember, when I was eleven or twelve, being staggered by the vividness of the sex scenes in *The God-father*, Puzo's novel. Of course, with Puzo, there was a food angle. Sonny Corleone possesses a penis so elephantine that his wife is ecstatic when he takes a mistress because, "after the first year my insides felt as mushy as macaroni boiled for an hour." Male writers have worked overtime to describe women's sexual parts, often in culinary terms. In London's *Times Literary Supplement*, John Updike was once taken to task for trying too hard to compare a nipple and a dried apricot. D. H. Lawrence compared the "wonderful moist conductivity" of a fig to a woman's genitals.

Sometimes you're alone at the table, or in the bedroom. The most infamous scene in American literature may be the one

---

* The poet Thom Gunn, in his letters, prints this joke: "Jeffrey Dahmer to Lorena Bobbitt: 'You're not going to leave that, are you?'"

† "After Reading *Mickey in the Night Kitchen* for the Third Time Before Bed."

in *Portnoy's Complaint* in which Alexander Portnoy . . . well, let's let him tell it. "I believe that I have already confessed to the piece of liver that I bought in a butcher shop and banged behind a billboard on the way to a bar mitzvah lesson. Well, I wish to make a clean breast of it, Your Holiness. That—she—it—wasn't my first piece. My first piece I had in the privacy of my own home, rolled round my cock in the bathroom at three-thirty—and then had again on the end of a fork, at five-thirty, along with the other members of that poor innocent family of mine. So. Now you know the worst thing I have ever done. I fucked my own family's dinner." People forget that Alex also has sexual congress with a cored-out apple, and an empty milk bottle. A scene to rival it appears in Viet Thanh Nguyen's *The Sympathizer*. His protagonist commits an unnatural act with a gutted squid he steals from his mother's kitchen.

\* \* \*

At some point, eating out, the check will arrive. Some nights it's a painful moment. We get into scrapes, Cree and I, scrapes that leave us quaking at how we've flirted with disaster. A few years ago, we were at a birthday dinner for an old friend, at a lauded new restaurant in lower Manhattan. We and another couple were, by tradition, buying his birthday meal. It was a funny, talkative, extended, candlelit, fairly Lucullan night. As the cocktails and wine bottles and dessert plates and port glasses piled up, I began to realize that our cut of the bill was likely going to hit $500, which was about what we had on our last working debit card.

This is probably the place to interject that my favorite writer, when it comes to the "evil moment" of requesting a restaurant bill, is Max Beerbohm, the great British satirist. In one essay he talked about hosting a bistro dinner and wondering if he'd be able to pay for it. "I never let this fear master me," he wrote. "I never said to anyone 'Will you have a liqueur?'— always 'What liqueur will you have?' But I postponed as far as possible the evil moment of asking for the bill. When I had, in the proper casual tone (I hope and believe), at length asked for it, I wished always it were not brought to me *folded* on a plate, as though the amount were so hideously high that I alone must be privy to it."

I should add, too, that splurging $500 on dinner is, for us, a rare event but not completely unheard-of. I'm in sympathy with Jim Harrison, who wrote that "whereas five hundred bucks seems reasonable for a great meal, I would not conceive of spending that much for an article of clothing or footwear." We all have our priorities. At our dinner, we hadn't yet asked for the check, folded or unfolded. I looked across at Cree and wrinkled my forehead, making the universal face for "what the hell are we going to do?" She tapped her watch and rolled her eyes toward a clock against the rear wall. I knew instantly what she meant. It was late on a Wednesday night. I get paid on Thursdays, sometimes at the stroke of midnight. This was only an hour away! All we had to do was order more port and settle in. Alas, the others were drunk and restless. There was no keeping them at the table. We put our Visa card down and tightened our sphincters. It went through.

Now that I'm in my late fifties, I think a lot about how, as Harrison once wrote, I am about to round third base in life—and home plate is a hole in the ground. Nora Ephron wrote that none of us should wait to have our "last meal." Have it now, have it all the time, or you may end up in the ICU and your last meal will be institutional porridge. Last meals are a good dinner-table topic. (So is the question, "If you could only eat in one restaurant, lunch and dinner, for the rest of your life, what would it be?" I like brasseries, for their variety, for their rosy lighting, and for the *frites*, and I tend to answer, because it is tried and true: "Balthazar" in Manhattan.) I used to think I'd want an orgiastic feast at my last meal, like the one François Mitterrand, the former French president, in old age, was said to have consumed the evening before he planned to stop eating altogether. Mitterrand had oysters and capon and foie gras, in quantity, and finally a rare delicacy, ortolans—the songbirds one consumes whole, with a white cloth over the face, to hide one's shame of eating it from God. Ortolans are endangered, and consuming them has been illegal in the EU since 1979.

Over time, I have mentally pared my wishes down. I'd want the great and familiar. Two martinis, then a first course: mozzarella and tomato, as selected by Cree, who knows what she is doing with basil and olive oil and salt. Then a roast chicken, perhaps with onions and carrots and sausages and Halloumi tucked into the roasting pan, with *frites* and asparagus. A bottle of wine finer than the decent but unobtrusive bottles we drink nightly. I don't have a sweet tooth, so no dessert. *Et voilà*, I'm fortified for my walk to home plate.

On his deathbed, Clark Gable asked for chili from Chasen's, the West Hollywood restaurant that closed in 1995. Orwell died with his favorite fishing rods in his hospital room. Joseph Mitchell, the *New Yorker* writer, said that when death was too much on his mind, he would wake early and walk to the Fulton Fish Market on the East Side riverfront. I used to walk there, too, when I was young in Manhattan, and watch the fishmongers carve and weigh whole tuna. It was worthy of Zola, of Les Halles. It reeked, beautifully. It closed in 2005, and later reopened in the Bronx.

It's hard to feel modern, Knausgaard wrote, when death is all around us. Food is part of how we cope. "When someone dies, I was taught growing up in California, you bake a ham," Joan Didion wrote in *The Year of Magical Thinking*. After her husband, the writer John Gregory Dunne, died, she wrote that "I will not forget the instinctive wisdom of the friend who, every day for those first few weeks, brought me a quart container of scallion-and-ginger congee from Chinatown. Congee I could eat. Congee was all I could eat." What can we do, in the face of death, but go on living? In Isaac Bashevis Singer's beautiful short story "The Cafeteria," the narrator, a writer, eats many of his meals in a cafeteria on Manhattan's Upper West Side. He meets other Russian and Polish immigrants there. It's a winding story about a woman who survived the Russian death camps and comes to think she saw Hitler in the cafeteria the night it burned down. The moment in Singer's story that stays with me is one in which the narrator talks about what it's like to have his aged crowd disappear, picked off by death, one by one. "Each time, I am startled, but at my age one has to be ready for such tidings," he says. "The food sticks in the throat; we look at each other in confusion, and our eyes ask mutely, Whose turn is next? Soon we begin to chew again. I am often reminded of a scene in a film about Africa. A lion attacks a herd of zebras and kills one. The frightened zebras run for a while and then they stop and start to graze again. Do they have a choice?"

One of my models, if I am lucky enough to reach late old age, will be Jessica Mitford. She was in her late seventies when she learned she had an aggressive form of cancer and a short time to live. Mitford decided, since she was dying anyway, she would thenceforth eat nothing but chocolate mousse. Her great friends, including Maya Angelou, came to sit at her bedside. Philip Roth, in *The Dying Animal*, was talking about everything—sex, food, books, experience—when he wrote, "Of what do you ever get more than a taste? That's all we're given in life, that's all we're given of life. A taste. There is no more."

My desire to eat while I read, and to keep a sentry lookout for the food in literature, has hardly diminished with time. If anything, my affliction has worsened. Deep down I'm still that chunky kid who bicycled home and threw all the newspapers on the floor and went to make a monster sandwich and then fell on it all. These days my back won't permit me to lie on the floor for long. But I still know I'm reading something sensational when I make multiple trips from the couch to the kitchen to keep the combinatory pleasure flowing. These have been some of the great moments of my life and, thinking about them now, I can almost taste them.

# ACKNOWLEDGMENTS

Thank you to Daniel Okrent, Max Watman, Cree LeFavour, Harriet LeFavour, Valentina Rice, and John Stinson for their wise input. Thank you to Jonathan Galassi and Katherine Liptak at Farrar, Straus and Giroux for their steady guidance, as well as to the production editor, Bri Panzica; the cover designer, June Park; and the interior designer, Gretchen Achilles. At *The New York Times*, where some of this material originally appeared in different form, thank you to John Williams, Emily Eakin, Dave Kim, Pamela Paul, and Gilbert Cruz. At *Esquire*, where a portion of this material originally appeared in different form, thank you to Jay Fielden and Michael Hainey. Thank you to my agent, David McCormick. Thanks also to Petite Clouet Café in New Orleans, where a section of this book was written. Thank you, finally, to the Naples High School English department circa 1982, especially Jack Morris, Richard Brandon, Janet Claire Bagg Freisenbruch, Donald Glancy, and Kathy Fearon.

# INDEX

# PERMISSIONS ACKNOWLEDGMENTS